LEGAL AND ETHICAL DICTIONARY FOR MENTAL HEALTH PROFESSIONALS

C. Emmanuel Ahia

University Press of America,® Inc.
Lanham · New York · Oxford

Copyright © 2003 by
University Press of America,® Inc.
4720 Boston Way
Lanham, Maryland 20706

PO Box 317
Oxford
OX2 9RU, UK

All rights reserved
Printed in the United States of America
British Library Cataloging in Publication Information Available

ISBN 0-7618-2508-8 (clothbound : alk. ppr.)
ISBN 0-7618-2509-6 (paperback : alk. ppr.)

<u>DEDICATION</u>

To my wife and life partner, Dr. Ruth N. Ahia and our four kids:
IJ, Chichi, Chidinma and Chuks.

Contents

Preface

In the middle of class discussion in the Spring Semester of 2001, Valerie J. Kerrigan, a student in my class, "Legal and Ethical Issues in Counseling and Psychotherapy," asked if there was any dictionary that could help her understand with greater clarity, the meaning of the numerous legal and ethical terms involved in the course. I do not remember my exact answer, neither does she. But the idea of a legal and ethical dictionary for mental health professionals was there and then born. Fortunately, I had just completed a sabbatical in the Fall Semester of 2000, reviewing approximately 300 mental health related cases litigated and/or reported in jurisdictions across the United States. The purpose of the review was to conduct an analysis of these cases, identify areas and issues where psychotherapists remain most lawsuit vulnerable, and based on the findings, develop a legal auditing system that will help mental health agencies and professionals maintain compliance with legal and ethical standards.

The case law analyses clearly showed that one reason why mental health professionals find themselves in violation of legal and ethical standards is that they do not know or understand the exact meaning of legal or ethical terminologies on which they based a professional action or behavior. In *Runyon v Smith* (2000), for example, New Jersey Supreme Court found that psychologist, Maureen B. Smith, Ph.D. breached psychologist-patient privilege when she testified that her client Diana Runyon was a "danger" to her children. Dr. Smith had assumed she had a "duty to warn" and protect the children but it clearly did not appear that she knew or understood the legal meaning of duty to warn. Cases of this nature abound.

Given the above, I became convinced that a Legal and Ethical Dictionary that concisely defines and/or explains legal and ethical words and terminologies, would become a good desk reference for practicing mental health and forensic professionals who are not lawyers. It should help a professional understand the general legal and ethical definition and meaning of a terminology. While the application of the definition to different fact patterns in different cases and jurisdictions may lead to variable results, it remains important, indeed critical, that professional behavior and action be predicated on a thorough understanding of the definition of the legal terminology involved. Without this understanding, contextualization to variable facts and different jurisdictions is bound to be more complicating.

The head words and phrases were selected from a review of fifty books and articles on mental health law and ethics. Effort was made to define and/or explain terminologies and phrases in ways that they can be easily applied to situations encountered frequently by mental health professionals. They were also kept short and concise. I carefully avoided the influence of any single case from a single jurisdiction, in order to make the baseline meanings generally applicable. I also took the liberty to introduce terms that may help clarify different definitions and conditions.

The main section of the dictionary contains 670 entries, A - Z. This is followed by Appendix A – D. Appendix A contains the most recent ethical codes of American Counseling Association (ACA 2002), Ethical Principles of Psychologists and Code of Conduct of American Psychological Association (APA 2002), American School Counselors Association (ASCA 2002), the Code of Ethics of the American Association for Marriage and Family Therapy (AAMFT, 2001), and Code of Ethics of National Association of Social Workers (NASW 2002). Appendix B a list of state professional licensure boards with their phone and fax numbers, and E-mails. It is hoped that this will facilitate a contact that would be useful to professionals. Appendix C lists some frequently used mental health acronyms, while Appendix D is a list of the Websites of 95 specialized mental health fields and/or professions.

I am indebted to many individuals and circumstances for this production. First and foremost, I am grateful to attornies James Castagnera, and Theodore Remley for their preview and review of the manuscripts, and Arnold Samet for a last minute check for errors and "typos." I specifically thank Daniel A. Martin for his work on the Website component, Geraldine Panzera for both dutiful typing of the Manuscript and helping with the Copyright permissions, Cherry Oakley, with whom I identified and organized the words and phrases to be included in the dictionary. Paul Causton was helpful in putting together the Appendix on the State Licensure Boards. Our department secretary, Colleen Martin, is thanked here for her typing of the book proposal and helping with initial correspondence with the publisher. Michele Figueroa demonstrated a high level of competence and dedication in getting the final manuscript ready for publication. For that, I thank her. I finally must confess that this dictionary and my other professional activities happen in the congenial and highly supportive working environment here at Rider University Graduate department of Education and Human Services.

Lawrenceville, New Jersey   C. Emmanuel Ahia
September, 2002

A

A Priori

A reasoning process that lead to a conclusion about something by assuming that it logically must flow from previously established fact. For Example: "Ed had his *two* *feet* amputated when he was a child, and has been in a wheelchair ever since. Thus one can assume *a priori* that he was not the bandit observed *running* from a crime scene."

Abandonment

Unilateral severance by a mental health professional of the professional services and relationship between the professional and a client without reasonable notice at a time when the patient still needs continuing care. Or discontinuation of needed services without provision of or referral to adequate alternative treatment.

Abortion

Premature termination of pregnancy at a time when the fetus is capable or incapable of sustaining life independent of the mother.

Abuse Allegation

A charge that someone has abused a member of a legally protected class (a child or the elderly). Allegations may lead to a parent of the children or the victim being excluded from the home. It may also lead to an investigation, and/or to the removal of the alleged victim or child from the parent or custodian. It may lead to criminal prosecution in all states that have anti-abuse laws.

Abused Adult

An adult for who there exists reasonable suspicion that he or she has been abused in violation of state law. The abuse may be physical, sexual, emotional, economic, and social. The age required for an abuse allegation depends on state or federal law.

Abused/Neglected Children

Children for whom there exists reasonable suspicion of any form of abuse or neglect in violation of state or federal law.

Accreditation

A process whereby an academic institution or professional program voluntarily undergoes review by a recognized accrediting body. Accreditation is usually a stamp of approval and a statement about the quality of an institution's degrees or programs.

Professional accreditation ensures that an educational program or process meets high standards of practice. Examples of accrediting bodies are APA, CACREP, ACSW. Educational program accredited by these bodies tend to have high standards for professional training beyond standards required for offering a degree. For legal purposes however, being certified or licensed and in good standing gives a professional more credibility.

Actionable

Giving rise to a "cause of action." Something or situation for which one may file suit.

Actus Reus

The behavioral part of a crime; that which is physically done. See '*mens rea*', which is the mind set or the mental process required for a crime (eg. "knowingly," "wantonly"). The thinking behind a crime or the thinking which preceded a criminal act.

Administrative Agency

Any branch or division of the government other than the judicial or legislative branches (such as the Social Security Administration, Veterans Administration, or the Department of Agriculture). Government body charged with administering or implementing particular groups of legislation.

Admissibility (of evidence)

Refers to the issue of whether a court, applying the rules of evidence, is bound to receive or permit introduction of a particular piece of evidence. Admissible evidence is that which meets the requirements of the law of evidence.

Administrative Law

Regulations and procedures that govern the operation of administrative agencies.

Adoption

The legal voiding or cancellation of ties to biological parents and the creating of new legal ties to adopting parents.

Advance Directives

Written instructions expressing person's health related wishes in the event that he or she becomes incapacitated and is unable to make such decisions for himself or herself. This may or may not include a durable power of attorney (DPA) which authorizes a specific person to make those decisions.

Adversarial System (Process)

A System of law in the United States whereby the truth is thought to be best revealed through a contest in the courtroom between opposite sides to a dispute.

Adverse Drug Reaction

Unusual or unexpected response to a normal dose of a medication, prescription or nonprescription. An injury caused by the use of a drug in the usual, acceptable fashion.

Advisory Opinion

An opinion rendered by a court when no actual case is before it. Although some state courts render advisory opinions, the United States Supreme Court and lower federal courts do not.

Advocacy

The active espousing of a legal case. The professional duty a lawyer has in the representation of a client. In legal proceedings, mental health expert witnesses should not really be their clients advocates, but should instead present their (expert) opinions objectively. This is different from the duty of advocacy expected when a treating clinician acts in the interests of his or her patient/client.

Affidavit

A voluntary statement of fact, or a voluntary declaration in writing of facts, that a person swears or affirms to be true before an official authorized to administer an oath.

Affirm

To uphold a lower court's decision, ruling, or judgment.

Affirmative Defenses

Defenses deemed lawful in a given set of facts. Defenses recognized by the law which when introduced by defendants in a trial, will reduce or eliminate responsibility for acts. In such situations, the defendants normally have the burden of proof. Examples are the "self-defense," "heat-of-passion," and "victim of abuse" defenses. All these defenses try to prove that the defendant had a legitimate reason for committing an illegal act.

Agency Liability

A legal theory holding that all persons in an "agent" relationship can be vicariously liable for each other's official acts. This is often the case in partnerships or arrangements where two of more professionals go into business as partners. See *Vicarious Liability*.

Agent

A person who acts on behalf of another, or an organization with a mutual agreement to do so. A legal representative.

Alienation of Affections

A tort (civil wrong) arising from the willful and malicious interference with a marriage relationship by some third party. Abolished in many states, it still may be raised in some when therapy (or a therapist) is accused of interfering with a patient's marriage.

Alimony

Payments to a spouse. This may be temporary alimony ("alimony pendente") or permanent alimony. Temporary alimony is used by courts when the dependent spouse needs time and training to become self-supporting. Permanent alimony is usually ordered by courts when the supported spouse is unable to become self-supporting. See *Spousal Support*.

Allegations

Claims that a person has violated a law or is liable for wrongfully harming another person financially or personally. The charges in a criminal indictment and the accusations in a civil complaint are allegations.

Alternative Dispute Resolution (ADR)

An alternative to the adversary system or litigation in a court of law. Mediation and arbitration are examples.

American Counseling Association (ACA)

The largest professional group representing Counselors (formerly American Association for

Counseling and Development). The largest single organization of mental health professionals.

American Psychological Association (APA)
The largest professional group representing psychologists. APA also refers to The American Psychiatric Association. See *American Psychological Society (APS)*. APS is a splinter organization representing academic psychologists.

Americans with Disabilities Act (ADA)
Federal Act that bars employers from discriminating against disabled person in hiring, promotion, or other provisions of employment, especially in the provision of reasonable accommodation in response to their disability.

Amicus Curiae "friend of the court."
An outside person or organization (i.e., one not involved as a litigant) who brings a matter of interest to the court's attention when it might otherwise be overlooked. (Note that this phrase does not apply to expert or fact witnesses). A friend of the court. One who has an indirect interest in a case and offers or is requested to provide information to the court in order to clarify particular matters before the court. A position paper filed in court by such a person or organization is called "Amicus Curiae brief."

Amnesia
A medical or psychological condition of forgetfulness. A mental condition that creates an inability to recall all or relevant aspects of an event. A loss of memory which if unaccompanied by any other disorder, will be rejected by most courts as adequate ground upon which to base a finding of incompetency.

Anatomical Doll
Human-looking doll (toy) used during interviews by various professionals to help children communicate more objectively and effectively in cases of abuse either through a child's interaction with the doll or a demonstration of interpersonal occurrences. Use of these dolls can become controversial mostly because of its potential for mis-use in child sexual abuse cases.

Annulment
A legal or religious decree that a marriage never existed. An annulment proceeding is a court hearing to determine whether an annulment should be granted.

Answer
The first pleading by the defendant in a lawsuit. This statement sets forth the defendant's responses to the charges contained in the plaintiff's "complaint."

Antenuptial Agreement
A contract between future marriage partners to determine the partners' rights during and/or after the marriage. Also called a "premarital

contract" or "prenuptial contract or agreement."

Appeal

An application to a higher court to reject, amend or rectify a lower court's ruling.

Appellate Court

A higher court whose jurisdiction allows it to review cases already tried in a lower court. (Note that an appeal is not a new trial, but a review of the legal matters involved in a previous one. The appellate court may sometimes authorize a new trial in a *trial* court).

Appellee

The party who defends against an appeal. Usually the party that may be satisfied with the immediate prior ruling in a judicial process. A person or party against whom an appeal is brought by the appellant.

Apportion

The ability to go beyond factual "knowing" to useful understanding, as in a mentally ill person's ability to appreciate the difference between right and wrong, not merely to quote it. To assign.

Arbitrary

An act or action taken without a fair and substantial cause. Guided by will or emotion only rather than facts and reason. Illogical, indefensible given the set of facts available; deviation from tradition without justification. Note: Counselors whose treatment of clients fall outside established professional traditions can be accused of being professionally arbitrary and/or capricious. (See *Capricious*).

Arbitration

An alternative dispute resolution process occurring outside a courtroom; usually less formal and less costly than trial. Arbitrators make decisions that may or may not be binding on participant. Decisions made in "Binding Arbitrations" are binding on participants.

Arraign

To accuse of a wrong. *Arraignment* is the first step in the criminal accusation process, at which the defendant is formally charged and presented with an "accusatory instrument," informed of his/her rights, offered an opportunity to plead, provided with counsel if he or she can afford none.

Artificial Insemination

The fertilization of a female with sperm from a sperm donor by mechanical means.

Aspirational Ethics or Professional Standards

Standards (beyond those mandated by professional ethics), deemed by a profession to be compatible and/or consistent with the production of positive and healthy results for clients, counselors, and the mental health professions as a whole. Lateness to counseling sessions and meetings or gross disregard of one's personal hygiene during professional engagements are not consistent with positive aspirational ethics.

Assault

A threat to use physical force on another person. Putting another in immediate apprehension of harm or offensive contact.. An intentional act designed to make the victim fearful and reasonably apprehensive of harmful or offensive contact.

Assessment (individual)

A process involving the collection and evaluation of information to address a client's counseling or rehabilitation concern or problem. Typically, an individual is assessed against a normative standard, or a set of criteria, for diagnosis, case management, planning, or treatment. Objective and/or projective testing may be involved.

Assignment

Transfer of rights, responsibilities, or property from one party to another. Assignee is a person to who those privileges are assigned or given. Assignor is a person who does the assigning.

Assumption of Risk

An act in which the injured party knows he or she might be injured and voluntarily places himself or herself at risk anyway. (That includes, for example, the patient who refuses an assessment or treatment procedure after the risks of not having it done have been appropriately explained. The person's assumption of the risks of not having the procedure is a

defense that the clinician may raise in any later negligence [e.g., malpractice] suit related to the person not receiving the procedure or treatment.

At-Fault

A judgment of legal liability against a person. In some states, fault is taken into consideration in divorce proceedings. Sometimes divorces are granted to an innocent spouse against an at-fault spouse. The fault analysis justified giving property and support to the innocent spouse. See *No-Fault Divorce*.

Attachment Theory

A psychological theory that maintains that the basis of parent-child attachments is influenced by innate variables and that many responses of infants, such as crying, are innate instead of learned. This theory is the reason why court tended to grant physical child custody more to mothers than fathers.

Attestation

Act of witnessing a document in writing.

Attorney Fees

Money paid to an attorney for legal representation

Autonomy

Right of an individual to make his or her own independent decisions. The principle which involves the affirmation of a person's individuality and the right to self determination, freedom to make choices, and freedom from the control or undue influence of others.

Aversive Stimulus
A painful or unpleasant stimulus used for punishment or for other forms of behavioral modification. Therapists who frequently use this type of technique need to be careful and ensure that they understand their state law on abuse.

B

Balancing
The weighing of opposing principles in an effort to or for the purpose of making the best judgement.

Battered Child Syndrome
Psychological or behavioral conditions resulting from a systematic abuse of a child. Evidence of an abnormal set of emotional, physical, and behavioral reactions or adaptations shown by a child, that will not occur but for the antecedent child abuse.

Battered Wife (Woman's) Syndrome
Psychological or behavioral conditions resulting from systematic spousal abuse. Abnormal set of irresistible emotional and behavioral reactions or adaptations to spousal abuse which will not occur but for the antecedent spousal abuse.

Battered Person Syndrome
Psychological and behavioral conditions resulting from

systematic dehumanization, oppression, bullying, intimidation and marginalization. Abnormal set of emotional and behavioral reactions or adaptation to systematic social and/or interpersonal maltreatment which will not occur but for the antecedent maltreatment/abuse.

Battery
Intentional harmful or offensive touching of one person by another without the consent of the person being touched. Battery need not result in physical injury, and may exist even if only an extension of a person is touched (e.g., plaintiff's car). Without informed consent, treatment is battery. See *Informed Consent.*

Behavior Modification
An application of the techniques of learning theories about conditioning to the prediction, change and/or control of behavior. When deprivation or an aversive stimulus is used with humans it is considered an extreme treatment.

Belmont Report
Report developed for Congress by the National Commission for the Protection of Human Subjects in Biomedical and Behavioral Research. See *Helsinki Report.*

Benevolence
A tendency on the part of a person to care, share, help and act generously toward others. Being altruistic.

Best Evidence Rule
Legal doctrine requiring that primary evidence of a fact (such as an original document) be introduced or that an acceptable explanation be given before a copy (rather than an original) can be introduced or testimony given concerning the fact.

Best Interest of the Child
A legal test applied in judicial or administrative proceedings affecting children, as in custody, adoption, termination of parental rights and child support hearing. A legal test that seeks to achieve the best result for a child involved in a judicial or administrative proceeding.

Beyond a Reasonable Doubt
The highest standard of proof required to convict a person of a crime. *Beyond a reasonable doubt* (~95%-98% probability that the crime was committed by this defendant) is used in only criminal cases. Clear and convincing evidence (~70% + probability) is the second tier used in both criminal and civil cases and proof "by a fair preponderance of the evidence" (>50% probability) is used exclusively in civil case. See *Clear and Convincing Evidence, Preponderance of the Evidence.*

Bifurcated Trial Procedure
Separated trial of particular but related issues in the same trial proceeding. For example, insanity of a defendant may be first tried and decided before the trial of other matters.

Bill
A formal written statement or complaint filed in a court. Also called pleading.

Binuclear Family
A family of divorce that has two parents who live in different residences and are both highly involved with the children. The children live in two nuclear families.

Biomedical Ethics
A way of understanding the complexity of biomedical advances and research in the light of religious or moral values. A process of humanization and justification of health care principles and practices.

Black Letter Law
A statutory law passed by a legislative body.

Bona Fide
Acting honestly and in good faith. In good faith, genuine, without fraud or deceit.

Breach
Failure to execute a legal duty.

Breach of Contract
A failure to perform a promise made in a contract and grounds for the other party to the contract to commence legal procedures. Failure to do that which a person has promise whether the agreement is written, verbal or implied-in-fact.

Breach of Duty
The failure by a professional to perform a legal duty imposed by

statute, case law, or professional ethics. This is one of the grounds for filing a tort lawsuit. See *Legal Duty; Tort*.

Brief
A written summary or condensed statement of a case. A written statement prepared by one side in a lawsuit to explain its case (legal points and authorities) to the judge.

Bubble of Confidentiality
The extension of confidentiality. When a professional consults with another professional of the same or different profession or with a paraprofessional, confidentiality is not destroyed. Instead it stretches (hence the term *bubble*) to cover all persons who participate in the consultation. The first professional must make all the others promise to honor confidentiality; he or she must not continue to use the services of anyone who does not agree to keep the materials or discussion confidential. Also called umbrella of confidentiality principle.

Burden of Proof
Requirement that facts asserted in a pleading be proved in accordance with rules of evidence by the person or persons making the assertions. The weight of the evidence that complainant, petitioner, or accuser must show to the trier of fact that the matter being considered actually occurred. In a criminal trial, the burden is "beyond a reasonable doubt" (extremely sure, generally 95-

98%); in most civil trials, a mere "preponderance of the evidence" (just over 50%); and in some civil settings, such as child custody and most civil commitments, "clear and convincing evidence is used.

Burnout
A feeling of physical and/or emotional exhaustion as a result of which a professional may show evidence of lowered interest, positivity, and productivity in his or her work or job.

C

Calumny
Slander, defamation, false prosecution (an old term).

Canon
A rule of ecclesiastical law, but also a rule or standard of conduct adopted by a professional organization for its members.

Capacity
The ability to make a rational decision. An age or condition at which the law expects a person to have the ability to make a rational decision. See *Diminished Capacity*.

Capital Offense
(Capital murder, capital crime) An offense punishable by death.

Capricious
Changeable in purpose or view. Willful or wanton change of direction to achieve a hidden purpose. A change of mind,

tradition, purpose or policy without justification.

Captain of the Ship Doctrine

A doctrine making the physician responsible for the negligent acts of other professionals because he or she had the right to control and oversee the totality of care provided to the patient.

Career Counseling

Counseling that focuses on a certain realm of the client's life—the world of work.

Caregiver

One who provides care to a patient or client.

Case Citation

A means of describing where the court's opinion in a particular case can be located. It identifies the parties in the case, the text in which the case can be found, the court writing the opinion, and the year in which the case was decided. For example, the citation "*Homer v Long*, 599 A.2d 1193 (Md. App.1992)" is described as follows:

- *Homer v Long* identifies the parties involved in the lawsuit.
- 599 A.2d 1193 identifies the case as being reported in volume 599 of Atlantic Reporter, 2d Series at Page 1193.
- Md. App. 1992 identifies the case as being in the Maryland Court of Appeals in 1992.

Case Law

Judge – made laws derived from cases. Aggregate of reported cases on a particular legal subject as formed by the decisions in those cases. Legal precedents relevant to a law's interpretation in specific circumstances and jurisdictions. By establishing precedents upon which courts rely, case law provides a primary source of legal authority parallel to statutory law.

Case Management

A process of mental health care which primarily focuses on maintenance of the positive results of care. The use of therapeutic techniques, consultation, follow-up, testing and professional collaborations to avoid a client's decompensation or deteoriation.

Cause of Action

Facts sufficient to allow a lawsuit to proceed.

Certification

A voluntary means of identifying oneself as a trained and qualified specialist in counseling, psychology, or other professions. Certification usually requires the meeting of standards of expertise beyond those required for general practice, e.g. the National Board for Certified Counselors (NBCC) awards a certification "National Certified Counselor" (NCC) to candidates who meet its standards. Certified Professionals must usually complete a number of continued education units (CEU) to remain in good standing.

Certiorari

A judicial process whereby a case is moved from a lower court to a higher one for review. All proceeding records at the lower court are sent to the higher court.

Charitable Immunity

Legal doctrine that holds charitable institutions blameless for their negligent acts. In virtually all jurisdictions, charitable or non-profit institutions are held liable for both criminal acts and negligent civil wrong-doing, i.e., they are not immune.

Chemotherapy
(pharmecotherapy)

A treatment of the symptoms of mental disorder with psychoactive medication. A type of cancer treatment.

Child Abuse

Harmful conduct with a minor, including sexual, physical or emotional abuse, and/or severe neglect of a child's basic needs for food, clothing, shelter, and medical treatment. Child abuse is a crime and mental health professional must report it in accordance to their state law.

Child Protective Service

Administrative agency changed with implementing child abuse and child protection laws of a state. Administrative processes used in the protection of children in any state.

Child Sexual Abuse Accommodations Syndrome (CSAAS)

A clinical syndrome in which an abused child denies that the abuse occurs. Sometimes misused as a diagnostic tool. Also called "child abuse accommodation syndrome."

Child Support

The payments made by one parent to the other parent for the maintenance of a child of those parents.

Child Witness

A minor testifying in the legal system. Children may be required to testify in abuse and custody cases. There is a debate between those wishing to protect children from stress in courts and those concerned with justice and defendants' constitutional rights to confront his or her accuser.

Circumstantial Evidence

Evidence that indirectly tends to prove a main fact in question. Such evidence is open to doubt, since it is inferential—for example, a student seen in the vicinity of the locker room at the time of a theft but who was not actually caught with the missing item.

Civil Action

An action in court with the expressed purpose of gaining or recovering individual or civil Rights or Compensation. A non-criminal case.

Civil Court

A court that hears civil (noncriminal) lawsuits. Type of cases heard include family law, landlord-tenant, tort (personal injury), business disputes, and real estate.

Civil Law
Body of law that describes the private rights and responsibilities of individuals. It is that part of law that does not deal with crimes. It involves actions filed by one individual against another (e.g. actions in tort and contract). *Criminal Law* on the other hand deals with the obligation of citizens to obey laws intended to protect society.

Civil Rights Law
Specific group of laws that give or affirm specific civil rights for all or specific group of citizen (e.g. the Voting Rights Act, Civil Rights Act of 1964, Title VII). Wrongful commitment to a mental hospital is a violation of a clients civil and constitutional rights.

Class Action
Legal Action brought by one or more individuals on behalf of themselves and others who are affected by a particular illegal act.

Clear and Convincing Evidence
The second level of proof used in both civil and criminal cases. In civil cases where there is a potential for the loss of important right (e.g. parental rights). In some criminal cases where the potential for the loss of civil liberties is low. This is the standard used in hearings concerning involuntary confinement of the mentally challenged. See *Beyond a Reasonable Doubt and Preponderance of the Evidence*.

Clinical Model Modality
The theoretical model of the ideal professional behavior for psychotherapists. Core values include using techniques mainly derived by use of the scientific model to benefit clients and others as exhibiting caring and empathy.

Clinical Privileges
Permission granted by an institution to a qualified professional to perform professional duties. This usually requires, but is not limited to, the screening of qualifications, diploma, state licensure, past professional record, and other relevant factors.

Closed-Shop Contract
Labor-management agreement that provides that only members of a particular union may be hired.

Code
A collection of laws. Most states have an education code containing all laws directly relevant to education. A systematic compilation of statutes, usually incorporating an indexing procedure to facilitate location of pertinent provisions.

Code Pleading
A legal procedure used in Europe and former European colonies based on interpretation of statutory civil law. It is inquisitorial rather than adversarial. In facts pleading, the facts of a case are pled.

Codicil
A supplement to a will that changes the will in some way. Demands the same competence as the will itself.

Collateral Attack
An attempt to challenge the credibility or validity of a judicial processing based on related or incidental issues.

Common Law
A system of law in which legal principles are derived from usage and custom as expressed by the courts or case law rather than from statutes. A body of legal principles that have evolved and continue to evolve and expand from court decisions.

Comity
A courtesy extended by one state or jurisdiction to recognize the decisions of another with concomitant jurisdiction.

Comity Doctrine
The legal doctrine of reciprocal cooperation between sovereign states.

Commingling
The mingling of separate property. In family law, the mingling of separate and community property in community property states and of marital and nonmarital property in common law states. Commingling converts all the property to community or marital property and confuses their identity.

Common Law Marriage
A marriage formed by living together and acting as if married in the eyes of the community. Not allowed in most states.

Common Law State
A family law for all states that are not community property states

Community Property
Most property acquired during a marriage in community property states. This property is seen as belonging to a "marital community" and is usually divided evenly on divorce. Also called marital property.

Commutation
Substitution of a lesser criminal sentence for a greater one, as in commuting a sentence to "time served" or commuting a death sentence to some period of incarceration.

Compensatory Damages
Damages awarded to reimburse the injured party only for the actual loss incurred. Punitive or exemplary damages are not considered compensatory. Punitive damages are awarded to punish the defendant for the wanton, reckless, purposeful or repeated manner in which the crime was committed. Punitive damages are suppose to serve as a deterrent to future acts of similar nature.

Competence (client)
The capacity of clients to make decisions—a precondition to be able to consent autonomously to services. See *Capacity*. The ability to make a rational decision.

Competence (counselor)

A counselor's capability to provide a minimum quality of service and within the counselor's (and his profession's) scope of practice. A counselor's competence is usually measured (for legal purposes) by what other reasonably prudent counselors will do under the same circumstance.

Competency to Stand Trial

The ability of a person to understand and rationally participate in a court proceeding.

Competent

Capable of doing a particular thing. Competence is not generic, but is tied to the task to which it is being applied (e.g. competence to make a will, to stand trial, to consent to a particular treatment). Not legally disqualified or legally incompetent from making legal decisions, such as giving consents or being a participant in a legal proceeding. See *Incompetent*.

Complaint

A formal pleading to a court demanding relief as well as informing the defendant of the grounds of the suit. The defendant is expected to file an answer to a complaint.

Compos Mentis-Mentally competent

To be mentally competent.

Comprehension

Having sufficient information and being able to understand that information. This concept is important during *Informed*

Consent   A client's comprehension or understand-ing of the nature (risks and benefits) of services, is a prerequisite for effective voluntary consent.

Compulsory Therapy

Therapy initiated and/or demanded by a third party, usually as a form of rehabilitation or ongoing assessment of a client. *Mandatory Counseling* such as is required by many states for <u>DUI</u> violators.

Conclusion of Fact

A legal conclusion based solely on the facts and "natural reasoning" without relying on rules of law.

Conclusion of Law

A legal conclusion (by a judge) reached solely by the application of rules of law, regardless of the facts. Used when the ultimate conclusion cannot reasonably be reached by applying facts of the case (e.g. when there are insufficient facts).

Concurrent Validity

The extent to which a test predicts scores on another test which seeks to assess the same variables. This is a form of criterion-referenced validity.

Concurring Opinion

An opinion written by a judge expressing agreement with the majority's holding. However, the concurring judge may disagree with the majority's reasoning or discuss additional principles or points of law.

Confession

An admission of guilt. In order to be valid in a criminal court, a confession must be accompanied by a number of legal elements, such as competence to make a confession, understanding of one's rights, and voluntariness.

Confidential Communication

A disclosure by a person to another which is intended to remain secret. It may be legally defined and protected. It usually applies to communications between clients and professionals. See *Confidentiality*.

Confidentiality

The obligation of counselors and other mental health professionals to respect the privacy of clients by not revealing to others the information communicated to them by client during counseling sessions. Legal or content confidentiality carries the penalty of law should there be a breach of confidentiality. Professional (non-legal) or contact confidentiality does not carry the weight of law, but could attract sanctions by the professional associations or certifying organizations with which the professional affiliates. Contact confidentiality can become content confidentiality in cases where the mental health agency is homogeneous e.g. alcohol and drug abuse center. In these cases, breach of contact implies a breach of content. Contact refers to the fact that a client is contacting a counselor for services.

Confidential Information

Information received by a mental health professional acting in a professional role, from a client or research participant.

Conflict of Interest

A conflict between loyalties or duties to a client or multiple roles with a single client. See *Dual Relationship*

Conflict of Laws

An area of law dealing with the clarification of inconsistencies and differences in laws or jurisdictions as they apply to the rights of individuals in particular actions.

Congressional Record

Document in which the proceedings of Congress are published. It is the first record of debate officially reported, printed, and published by the federal government. Publication of the Record began March 4, 1873.

Consent

An agreement either to give up (waive) a legal right or to accept a legal liability. Valid consent requires voluntary agreement after full disclosure of relevant facts by a legally competent person. Valid consent has elements of knowledge (cf., "informed consent"), competence to make the consent, and voluntariness or freedom from undue influence.

Consent Decree

An agreement by parties to a dispute, although not properly a judicial sentence, is in effect an admission by them that the decree is a just determination of their rights based upon the facts of the case.

Conservator

A person appointed by a court as the legal representative of a mentally ill or incompetent person. A conservator of the estate has the power to protect and control the property of an incompetent person. A conservator has the power to restrict the movements and actions of an incompetent person, who becomes the ward of the conservator.

Conservatorship (of adults and minors)

The legal entity set up and administered by a conservator to protect and restrict an incompetent person.

Constitution

The supreme fundamental law of a nation or state. Provisions are included to establish and organize the government and to distribute, limit and prescribe the manner of the exercise of sovereign powers. Basic principles and rights of the citizenry are enumerated in a constitution.

Construct Validity

The extent to which a test measures the theoretical construct it is supposed to measure, estimated by looking at criterion-referenced validity.

Consultant

In mental health professions, a person called upon by a primary caregiver or professional to advise him or her regarding a patient or patient care. A formal arrangement that enable any mental health professional to obtain a second opinion, advice, or oversight on an issue from a knowledgeable competent colleague. The consultant's professional relationship is with the person who contracted for his or her services (the consultee), and not generally with the patient; thus a clinician-patient relationship may not form.

Consultation (professional)

A formal arrangement where a consulting mental health professional obtains a second opinion, advice, or supervision on an issue or issues of concerns from a knowledgeable, competent colleague.

Consultation Confidentiality

A professional understanding, contract or agreement which extends counselor-client confidentiality to the consultant.

Contempt of Court

A violation of a court order and the legal charges based on that violation. Contempt is punishable by fines and/or jail. A contempt citation is a legal notice to a party that he or she has violated the orders of a court and that penalties will be applied.

Content Validity

The extent to which a test's questions are samples of the skills or behaviors that the test is supposed to measure. Direct and cross-examination are permissible during litigation to verify the content validity of forensic psychological tests.

Contingency (contingent) Fee
In law or forensic professions, a fee for services that depends on the outcome of a case; usually unethical for forensic expert witnesses and consultants.

Contract
A legal agreement. It can be written, oral, or implicit in the parties' behavior. Any guarantee or warranty is a contract. To contract is to make an agreement. Failure to honor the agreement is a breach of contract and a potential reason for a lawsuit. The remedies for breach include performance and financial compensation.

Contract Law
Substantive law governing the formation and enforcement of contracts.

Contributory Negligence
Negligence by the injured party when combined with the negligence of the defendant resulted in the proximate cause of the injury. Contributory fault is a more contemporary legal doctrine that allows for the apportionment of damage based on the percentage of the fault of the parties. A 40% at-fault plaintiff will receive only 60% of the awarded damages.

Coroner
A public official who investigates and rules on causes and circumstance of death. A coroner need not be a physician.

Coroner's Jury
Special jury called by the coroner to determine whether evidence concerning the cause of death indicates that death was brought about by criminal means.

Corpus Delicti
"Body of Crime," a prima facie showing that a crime has been committed. In a prosecution for murder, for example, it means a showing that the death was due to a criminal act. Does not apply only to murder, and does not refer solely to a "dead body."

Counterclaim
Defendant's claim in opposition to a claim of the plaintiff.

Court Martial
A military tribunal with jurisdiction over crimes against the law of the Armed Services. There are several differences between civilian (criminal) courts and courts martial. Court martials, like all other U.S. courts, are subject to the U.S. Constitution.

Court of Record
A court whose actions are recorded, possessing the authority to levy sanctions in a particular case.

Credibility
A state of being believable or trustworthy.

Criminal Action
A court action, brought by the state, against one charged with an offense against the state. This type of action may result in a fine or incarceration of the defendant. Civil action may also be brought

against the accused by persons harmed as a result of the criminal act.

Criminal Court

A court that hears criminal cases. The party initiating the case is a government office and the defendant has allegedly violated laws.

Criminal Law

Division of the law dealing with crime and punishment. It involves a legal action filed by a state or by the United States against a particular individual or individuals.

Criminal Negligence

Reckless disregard for the safety of others. It is the willful indifference to an injury that could follow an act. Reckless disregard of a professional duty based in law, which results in harm to another. An example is the failure of a mental health professional to report child abuse which lead to the further abuse and harm to the child.

Cross-examination

In the adversary process the questioning by the opposing attorney of a witness for the other side, after the witness has testified. The opposing attorney is allowed to challenge the testimony by asking leading questions and seeking inconsistencies. Legal theorists see cross-examination as the great legal engine of finding the truth.

Cruel and Unusual Punishment

A flexible term usually taken to mean punishment found to be offensive to an ordinary person

(i.e., to ordinary society, not just to one person). A punishment that is cruel and unusual is forbidden by law.

Custodial Parent

The divorced parent with whom the children live and who is usually entitled to child support. The divorced parent who has physical custody.

Custody (Legal/Physical)

The care and control of a person or thing. Custody implies immediate charge and responsibility for the protection of the person or child in one's custody not absolute control or ownership. Generally refers to the rights and responsibilities of parents related to their children. Legal custody is right and responsibility of a parent to make decisions about a child's life. Physical custody is the right and responsibility of a parent to reside with a child.

Custody Dispute

A disagreement between parents over rights to their children.

Custody Evaluation

An examination of children's home environment and their relationships with their parents for the purpose of awarding custody to either or both of the parents. Evaluators are mental health professionals and many are court employees or court appointed and their evaluation reports are expected to be professional and objective.

Cybercounseling
Counseling on the internet. This practice remains controversial relative to issues of con-fidentiality and therapeutic relationship.

D

Damages
Compensation or indemnity claimed by the plaintiff or ordered by the courts for injuries sustained by plaintiff and resulting from wrongful acts of the defendant.

Danger to Self or Others
A designation indicating suicidal or aggressive threats or actions. Used as a legal test to determine if a person should be involuntarily confined and/or confidentiality breached.

Dangerous Client
A client who has been determined or deemed to be a danger to him or herself or others. The therapist has a duty to breach confidentiality and warn foreseeable victims or persons who can protect the client.

Date Rape
Rape by a dating partner. The rapist usually perceives the sex as consensual and the victim's resistance as game playing.

Daubert Test
A modern legal test for the admissibility of scientific evidence based on the U.S. Supreme Court case of *Daubert v Merrell Dow Pharmaceuticals* decided in 1994. It requires that proposed scientific evidence be developed by use of the scientific method (a criterion for reliability) and be helpful to the court (relevant). This test is more lenient than the previously accepted *Frye* test and is accepted by all federal and many state courts. See *Frye Test.*

De Facto (In fact.)
A situation that exists in fact whether or not it is lawful. *De facto* segregation is segregation that exists regardless of the law or the actions of civil authorities. The legal opposite is *De jure.*

De Jure (By right/law.)
A state of affairs that has the force of law behind it either in its creation, support, or maintenance. A state of affair sanctioned by a civil authority.

DeMinimis
Insignificant matters with which a court will not concern itself. A matter that has no relevance to a court's execution of justice.

De Novo
Anew, afresh, a second time. A second trial of a case that has been sent back from a high court for a new trial.

Debriefing
Informing previously deceived research participants about the true purpose of an experiment.

Deception
In research, giving misleading information to allow and experiment to be done. The participants must be told the truth at a subsequent debriefing. This

can violate "human-subject" research laws and professional ethics if done without authoritative approval.

Decision

A conclusion or judgment of a court, as opposed to the reasoning or opinion of the court.

Declaratory Judgment

A court's legal conclusion on matters of law affecting undisputed set of facts in which the rights of the parties are recognized or clarified.

Declaratory Relief

An opinion expressed by the court without ordering that anything be done as a matter of law; it recognizes the rights of the parties involved.

Decree

A court order issued in an equity suit.

Defamation Injury

Harm done to a person's reputation or character caused by the false statements of another made to a third person. Defamation can be libel (written) or slander (spoken). Erroneous diagnosis can be basis for a defamation suit against a therapist.

Defendant

In a criminal case, the person accused of committing a crime. In a civil suit, the party against whom the suit is brought.

Default Decree

A decree or order in favor of one side in a legal action, which is issued when the other side fails to appear at the appointed time.

Default Judgment

Refers to a judgment entered in the absence of a party to a case.

Deinstitutionalization

The release of persons from a mental institution. Usually by the order of a court or a civil authority.

Delayed Discovery Rule

A lenient rule of evidence, which says when evidence not timely discovered or known can still be of legal usefulness. The starting time of the statue of limitations period. The time within which a lawsuit must be filed because it is at that time that evidence of injury was actually discovered. This rule has great significance for cases in which sexual abuse is discovered by memory recovery techniques during therapy years after the abuse.

Demurrer

An allegation by a defendant admitting that although the facts are correct, a suite is not justified nor do they require an answer by the defendant because there are no legal issues created by the facts.

Dependent Child

A child who has been made a ward of the courts or a child owed support by parents.

Deponent

A witness who gives information under oath during a deposition.

Deposition

A method of pretrial discovery that consists of statements of fact taken by a witness under oath in a question and answer format as it would be in a court of law with opportunity given to the adversary to be present for cross examination. Such statements may be admitted into evidence if it is impossible for a witness to attend a trial in person.

Developmentally Disabled

A condition marked by subnormal abilities; similar to mentally retarded, but usually connoted more selective deficits.

Dictum (obiter dictum)

An opinion expressed by a judge in a proceeding that is not necessary in formulating the court's decision. It therefore, does not establish binding precedent. However, it may indicate the judge's persuasion. A digression or discussion of related points that do not go to the heart of the case at hand.

Differential Diagnosis

The process whereby one mental disorder is used to describe a client or another disorder with similar diagnostic signs, symptoms, or course.

Diminished Capacity

A state of mental functionality that falls below a normal standard. A state of mental dysfunctionality, the basis of which a person may be disqualified from giving a legal testimony or bearing a legal responsibility.

Directed Verdict

When a trial judge decides either that the evidence and/or law is clearly in favor of one party or that the plaintiff has failed to establish a case and that it is pointless for the trial to proceed further, the judge may direct the jury to return a verdict for the appropriate party. The conclusion of the judge in such situation, must be so clear and obvious that reasonable minds could not arrive at a different conclusion.

Direct-Examination

The questioning of a witness in court by the side that called that witness to testify. It is usually followed by a cross-examination by the other side.

Disability

An identifiable condition that is medically or psychologically stable and whose functional limitations, when manifested, are recognized and for which appropriate or reasonable accommodation is warranted as a matter of law.

Discharge

A description of methods by which a legal duty is extinguished. Discontinuation of a legal obligation.

Discharge Summary (Termination Report)

A clinical record that summarizes a client's initial complaints, course of treatment, final diagnosis, prognosis and suggestions for follow-up care.

Disclaimer

The refusal to accept certain types of responsibility. For example, a college catalogue may disclaim any responsibility for guaranteeing that the courses contained therein will actually be offered, since courses, programs, and instructors are likely to change without notice.

Discovery
A pretrial evidence gathering process intended to ascertain those facts of a case not already admitted; it includes testimony and documents that may be under the exclusive control of the other party. Discovery facilitates out of court settlements. See *Deposition, Interrogatory, and Subpoena.*

Discretion
Reasonable exercise of power or right to act in an official capacity. In clinical settings, may be applied to a clinician-employee's freedom to act in a patient's best interest, or flexibility to make decisions regarding care. Involves choices made within professional parameters in which a counselor may exercise flexibility to act as he or she thinks best.

Discretionary Power
Exercise of judgment in deciding whether to take action in a certain situation.

Dismissal
A final disposition of a suit by a court by sending it out of court without a trial of the issues.

Dissenting Opinion
An opinion written by a judge in disagreement with the decision of the majority hearing a case.

Dissolution of Marriage
The name for divorce in some no-fault states such as California.

Diversion
Counseling offered as an alternative to incarceration. An example is that offered in some states to "driving under the influence (DUI)" offenders.

Divorce
The legal ending of a marriage.

Divorce Mediation
A negotiation or conflict resolution process by which a mediator helps a divorcing couple to develop and agree to a "written divorce agreement." Some states required divorcing couples to engage in divorce mediation.

Documentary Evidence
Documents and their contents admitted into evidence.

Domestic Violence
Violence between relatives or individuals who have recently lived together or are in a romantic relationship, either married or unmarried. Violence occurring among and within family relationships.

Do-Not-Resuscitate (DNR)
Directive of a physician to withhold cardiopulmonary resuscitation in the event a patient experiences cardiac or respiratory arrest. Such order must be in writing, signed and dated by the physician. For a DNR to be legal, appropriate consents must be obtained from the patient or his or her family or legal advocate.

Dowry

Common law rights of a wife to have the use of a specified percentage of her ex-husband's property for the remainder of her life. Money or goods paid or presented to a bride's family before marriage is approved in some countries.

Drug Addiction

A condition of being physically and/or psychologically dependent on and usually craving for a drug or drugs.

Dual Relationship

Acting in more than one role with another person. The existence of a professional or clinical relationship in addition to or alongside of (social, business, or personal) non-professional relationship. A therapist who owns a house with a client is involved in the client-therapist relationship and the business partner relationships. Not all dual relationships are wrong or conflicting but all carry the risk of abuse/misuse of power, or loss of objectivity. Dual relationships can be conflicting or complimentary. Conflicting dual relationships (boundary violations) refer to those in which the professional and non-professional relationships conflict and the loss of clinical objectivity is unavoidable. Complimentary dual relationship (boundary crossing) refers to those in which the client benefits (and loses nothing) as a result of being involved in a professional and non-professional relationship with a counselor.

Due Care (Professional)

A standard of care or legal duty owned to clients below which a practicing mental health professional will be held legally liable if mishap or injury occurs. The expected level of care the absence of which defines negligence. The occurrence of injury is not in itself evident of negligence. Only when the treatment rendered did not demonstrate the knowledge and skill required of a reasonably prudent practitioner.

Due Process

The right a person has to be given notice of adverse legal actions and to a hearing to defend against them. Due process rights primarily arise from the Fifth, Sixth, Thirteenth, and Fourteenth Amendments to the U.S. Constitution. As the practice of mental health professionals becomes more legalized, due process becomes more important. Treatment of mental patients and special education of special needs children both require that the practitioner observe due process principles.

Due Process of Law

The implication that the powers of government are exercised similarly in similar situations in order to protect individual rights. Denial of this right is prohibited by the Fifth and Fourteenth Amendments when life, liberty or property are involved.

Durable Power of Attorney
Legal instrument enabling an individual to act on another's behalf. In the health care setting it includes the authority to make medical decisions for another.

Duress
External influence over an action, such as to force one to commit an otherwise criminal act or influence one to consent to a clinical procedure. Duress is deem by law to remove the voluntariness necessary for an act, such as consent. Duress removes the intent necessary to define a criminal act.

Durham Rule (Test) (Also Product Rule)
A rule for determining criminal responsibility in persons with mental disease or defect, now used in few, if any jurisdictions. It was quite liberal, allowing for lack of responsibility if the act was simply the "product" of the mental disease or defect. See *Insanity Defense*.

Duty
An obligation of a conduct owed by one person or entity to another. In the law of negligence (including malpractice), a duty is a legal obligation for which breach results in liability. Mental Health Professionals must, therefore, conduct themselves in such a manner as to avoid negligent injury to those to whom they owe a duty or have a therapeutic or other professional relationship.

Duty to Predict
A duty based on the special relationship of a therapist and client that requires the therapist to predict whether the client is a danger to self or others. A client's past behavior is one way to predict dangerousness.

Duty to Prevent Harm
A duty based on the special relationship of a therapist and client that requires the therapist to take steps to prevent a client from committing suicide or other injury to self or others.

Duty to Protect
A counselor's responsibility to protect the intended victims of a dangerous client. A counselor's responsibility to protect a client and others from foreseeable outcome of his or her dangerous propensities.

Duty to Warn
A legal responsibility based on the special relationship of a therapist and client that requires the therapist to warn foreseeable victims of dangerous clients' intent and propensities. Also know as the Tarasoff Duty.

E

Electronconvulsive Therapy (ECT)
Passing an electrical current across the cerebral cortex to induce convulsions. This often reduces the symptoms of depression. With

overuse there are permanent memory deficits.

Emancipation

The process by which a minor achieves legal adult status for most purposes except for voting and alcohol use. Counselors must look to their state law for activities need for emancipation.

Emergency

Sudden unexpected occurrence or event causing a threat to life or health. The legal responsibilities of those involved in an emergency situation are measured according to the occurrence. Professionals responding to emergency are protected by Good Samaritan laws and the requirement of formally obtaining an informed consent from the client before providing services. A crisis management situation is an example.

En Banc

A proceeding in which all judges of a court participate in the decision.

Enabling Clause

A clause in a law empowering executive agencies to write regulations explaining the law. These then operate with the force of law and can be enforced by courts.

Enjoin

A legal process by which an individual or institution is required by a court of equity to cease or abstain from a particular action. See *Injunction*.

Equal Employment Opportunity Commission (EEOC)

A government agency set up by Congress to administer employment aspects of the Civil Rights Act of 1964, which forbids discrimination in the workplace

Equal Protection of the Law

A guarantee that no person or class of persons shall be denied the same protection of the laws that is enjoyed by other persons or classes in similar circumstances. Denial of this right is prohibited by the Fourteenth Amendment.

Equitable

Consideration of fault and fairness in most common law states.

Equity Law

A particular branch of law that differs from the common law. Primarily concerned with providing justice and fair treatment, equity law addresses issues the common law is unable to consider.

Erroneous Diagnosis

Diagnosis that is in error because it is not clinically defensible given known facts and data. Diagnosis that points away from where the known facts of a case will lead a reasonably prudent professional.

Estoppel

A legal prohibition from denying the truth of a point that has been established in case law, legislation, or one's own acts.

Et al (And others)

Indicates that unnamed parties are involved in the proceedings or writing.

Ethical Dilemma
Conflicts that arise when competing standards of right and wrong apply to a specific situation in counseling practice.

Ethical Principles
Higher order norms within a society consistent with its moral principles and which constitute higher standards of moral behavior or attitude. The application of ethical rules and principles to determine what is the right moral decision when an ethical dilemma arises. It focuses on the objective, rational, and cognitive aspects of the decision-making process.

Ethics
A branch of study in philosophy concerning how people ought to act toward each other, pronouncing judgments of value about those actions. A hierarchy of values that permits choices to be made based on distinguished levels of right and wrong. Ethics usually involves a judgment of human decisions or behaviors against an accepted standard primarily in non-religious context or situation.

Euthanasia
The intentional termination of life, also referred to as mercy killing or assisted suicide. Originally derived from two Greek words meaning "good death", it has come to mean death with dignity, or mercy killing of the hopelessly ill, injured or incapacitated.

Related Terms:
- Active Euthanasia occurs when a person intentionally commits an act that result in death.
- Passive Euthanasia occurs when life-saving treatment is withdrawn or withheld allowing a person to die.
- Voluntary Euthanasia occurs when the suffering incurable makes a decision to die, having made that decision when legally competent.
- Involuntary Euthanasia occurs when a person other than the suffering incurable makes the decision to terminate the life of an incompetent incurable or an unconsenting competent incurable.

Evidence
Anything presented as proof of a claim made in a legal proceeding. Anything legally presented at trial in a manner prescribed by law, to prove the assertions in a pleading.

Evidentiary Phase
The phase of a trial for the introduction of evidence. A trial begins with opening arguments, moves to the evidentiary phase (which normally takes most of the trial time), and may conclude with closing arguments.

Ex parte
A proceeding for the benefit of one party only.

Ex Post Facto
Generally referring to the fact that a criminal defendant must be tried under laws in force at the time of

the allegedly criminal act. Thus a person convicted of a murder committed when there was no death penalty cannot be sentence to death under a new law that allows it. It is important to understand that ex post facto applies only to criminal law, not civil matters.

Ex re.
Designates a private individual on whose behalf the state is acting in a legal proceeding.

Exception
An exemption from a law. Exceptions are written into laws defining situations in which the original laws do not apply. For example, client-therapist communications are normally confidential and protected but disclosures about child abuse are exceptions and must be reported to authorities.

Exclusionary Rule
A procedure in search-and-seizure cases seeking to suppress the use of evidence which has been improperly obtained. A legal principle that disallows the use of any evidence in legal proceeding if that evidence was obtained in violation of law.

Expert Testimony (opinion)
Testimony and opinion of a person skilled and knowledgeable in a relevant area, given to help a court and/or jury in deliberation and determination of the truth. An expert opinion can depend on education, training as well as on professional impressions and other out-of-court materials.

Expert Witness
Person who has special training, experience, skill, and/or knowledge in a relevant area and who is allowed to offer an opinion as testimony in court or a legal proceeding.

Expunge
Blot out. For example, a court order requiring that a person's record be expunged of any references to previous crime during or after a certain time period.

Extreme Treatment
A mental health treatment carrying a risk of harm such as electroconvulsive therapy. Special legal restrictions on use may apply in most jurisdictions.

Eyewitness
A witness who actually observes something. Much more perceptual and inaccurate than the legal system most times assumes.

Eyewitness Identification
A pretrial process that allows an eyewitness to a crime to point out the criminal in a photo-line-up.

F

Failure to Commit
A professional negligent act by a mental health professional who fails to institute procedures to involuntarily confine a client who turns out to be dangerous to self or others.

Fair Preponderance of the Evidence
A low burden of proof used only in civil law suits. The more-likely-than-not burden of proof requiring the production and proof of at least 51% of needed evidence.   See *Burden of Proof* and *Civil Law*

False Imprisonment
The intentional tort and a cause of action based on wrongful confinement of another without his or her consent. The confinement of another by force or intimidation thus denying him or her the liberty to move freely.

False Light
An intentional tort and a cause of action based on harm to a person's reputation and/or violations of privacy.

False Memory
A memory implanted by suggestion or some other source of subsequent information that did not originate in a real event. False memory is controversial in sexual abuse cases. See *High Suggestibility Theory*.

Family Law
The law of marriage, divorce, adoption, and related areas. A type of civil law.

Father Absence Syndrome
The collective harmful effects of absence of a father during children's development. Effects are different for girls and boys and for younger and older children. Common symptoms include guilt, depression, and anger. In some cases girls tend to show inappropriate behavior with males.

Father Custody
Custody of children by the father after a divorce.   See *Custody, Custody Dispute*.

Fault Doctrine
The legal doctrine holding that the innocent spouse in a divorce was the only one who could initiate the divorce and that the innocent spouse was entitled to property and support from the guilty spouse.

Federal Question
Legal question involving the U.S. Constitution or a statute enacted by Congress.

Federal Tort Claims Act
A federal law under which lawsuits for money damages against the federal government are heard, and a general waiver of sovereign immunity exist.

Felony
Serious crime usually punishable by imprisonment for a period of longer than one year or by death.

Fiduciary
The duty to keep safe and sound that which belongs to another. A relationship between persons in which one person acts for another in a position of trust. Mental health professionals have fiduciary responsibility for their client's information.

Finding
A conclusion of a court or jury regarding a question of fact or law.

Forbidden Zone

An area of prohibited conduct for professionals. Sexual relationship between psychotherapy clients and therapists is in the forbidden zone. Action in forbidden zones are considered boundary violations or conflicting dual relationships.

Foreseeability

A part of most legal tests for liability. If a danger is foreseeable, the professional should try to prevent it; failure to do so is negligence.

Foster Care

A government program that provides care and home for displaced and homeless children (and some disabled adults). An intermediate social program between loss of family care and permanent adoption of children.

Foundation of Evidence

A preliminary showing of fact that a proposed piece of evidence is likely to be relevant and reliable.

Four Level Model

A model of ethical practice which introduces an extended consideration of the contextual forces acting on ethical practice beyond the singular focus on the individual practitioner in relationship to the individual client.

Frye Test

The test of the admissibility of scientific testimony and procedures, based on *Frye v. United States* (1923), in which the court said that acceptance in the scientific community is essential before such evidence is accepted in the legal community. See *Daubert Test.*

G

Good Samaritan Laws

Laws designed to protect those who stop to render aid in an emergency. These laws generally provide limited immunity for specified persons from any civil suit arising out of care rendered at the scene of an emergency, provided that the one rendering assistance has not done so in a grossly negligent manner.

Governmental Function

A responsibility that is required of an agency for the protection and welfare of the general public.

Government Immunity

The doctrine that government entities are immune to lawsuits brought by private parties. It is now weakened and under attack. Also called "sovereign immunity."

Grand Jury

Jury called to determine whether there is sufficient evidence that a crime has been committed to justify bringing a case to trial. It is not the jury before which the case is tried to determine guilt or innocence.

Grandparent Visitation

The rights of grandparents to visit their grandchildren. Courts have been reluctant to grant these rights when both parents are opposed and it has been weakened by recent Supreme Court decisions.

Guardian

Person appointed by a court to protect the interests of and make decisions for a person who is incapable of making his or her own decisions.

Guardian Ad Litem

Literally, "Guardian for the litigation. A legal representative, usually an attorney, appointed by a judge to represent the interests of a person, such as a minor who is legally incompetent. The appointment is usually only for a specific legal case such as a custody trial involving allegations of child abuse. See *Legal Representative*.

H

Habeas Corpus

Literally, "Where is the body?" The great legal writ that asks whether a government has a legal reason or "body of evidence" to keep someone involuntarily confined. If mentally ill persons are not a danger to anyone and can provide for themselves, the government lacks a legal reason to keep them imprisoned or detained.

Harmless Error

Error of law that is not sufficiently prejudicial to warrant modification of a lower court decision by an appellate court.

Health Care Proxy

Document that delegates the authority to make one's own health care decisions to another adult, known as the health care agent, when one has become incapacitated or is unable to make his or her own decisions.

Health Maintenance Organization (HMO)

An organization that provides all or most required medical care for subscribers who make periodic payments. See *Managed Care* and *Preferred Provider Organization*.

Hearing

An oral proceeding before a court or quasi-judicial tribunal. A proceeding to ascertain to facts and provide evidence are labeled "trial-like hearings" or simply "trials." Hearings that relate to a presentation of ideas as distinguished from facts and evidence are known as "arguments." The former occur in trial courts and the latter occur in appellate courts. The terms *trial*, *trial-like hearing*, *quasi-judicial hearing*, *evidentiary hearing*, and *adjudicatory hearing* are all used by courts and have overlapping meaning.

Hearsay

Secondhand evidence; facts declared but are not in the personal knowledge of the witness but merely a repetition of what others said that is used to prove the truth of what is being contested. Hearsay is generally not allowed as evidence at a trial, although there are many exceptions.

Helsinki Declaration
An international declaration by the World Medical Association in 1967 and 1975 espousing the necessity for full informed consent as part of any biomedical research especially when children or incompetent persons are research subjects. This declaration did not cover behavioral research as was the case with Belmont Report. See *Belmont Report* and *Informed Consent*.

High Suggestibility Theory
The theory that most of the effects of hypnosis are the results of enhanced suggestibility. Seen by some professionals as a tool for implanting false memory. See *False Memory*.

Hired Gun (slang)
An expert hired by one side in a lawsuit who produces biased testimony favoring that side presumably because he or she was paid or bought.

Holder of Privilege
The person legally empowered to waive or assert a legal privilege against disclosure. Privileges are for the benefit of holders. The holder of the client-psychotherapist privilege is the client.

Holding
The rule of law in a case. That part of the judge's written opinion which applies the law to the facts of the case and about which can be said "the case means no more and no less than this." A holding is the opposite of a *dictum*.

Holographic Will
Will handwritten by the testator.

Homeless and Mentally Ill
Free mentally ill individuals living on the streets. Mentally ill persons not living at home or mental institutions.

Hospice
Long-term care facility for terminally ill persons. Usually provided in a setting more economical than that of a hospital or nursing home. Hospice care generally is sought after a decision has been made to discontinue aggressive efforts to prolong life. A typical hospice program includes as support services by trained individuals, family involvement, and control of pain and discomfort.

Hospital Privileges
The right of a professional to provide his or her services in or through a hospital. The right given to a professional to provide his or her services in or through an agency or institution. See *Clinical Privileges*.

Human Subjects Committee
A committee organized to review proposed research using humans as subjects (participants). The purpose of the review is to prevent ethical and legal violations. Human subjects committees may be organized on the level of a department or a whole institution. These committees typically have the power to stop research or to

require modifications in a research method.

Hypnosis

A technique that creates an altered mental state through clinically packaged suggestions. It has been frequently used as a memory-enhancement technique, with mixed results. See *High Suggestibility Theory* a n d *False Memory*.

Hypothetical

A set of background propositions read to an expert witness in a legal proceeding to allow the expert to render an opinion applicable to the facts of the current case.

I

Impairment

A condition that suggests a level of diminished function. For example, known prejudice or dual relationship can be deemed to impair the testimony of a mental health professional in any given case.

Impeach

To discredit testimony and the testifier. To show that testimony and a witness are not credible.

Impeachment

Legislative proceeding designed to remove an executive or judicial officer from office because of misconduct.

Impeachment of Experts

An attempt by the opposing lawyer to discredit an expert called to testify in a case. To render unreliable and legally useless the testimony of an expert witness.

Implied Contract

A perfectly legal contract that is created by expectancies and behaviors that lead the parties to believe they have an agreement. A valid contract that is inferred from the actions of the parties rather than being written or oral. A contract by custom.

In Camera

"In chambers"; in a judge's private office; a hearing in court with all spectators excluded. This can be done in the presence of opposing lawyers.

In Loco Parentis (In place of the parent)

A legal doctrine that assigns a parent's rights, duties, and responsibilities to others. The legal theory justifying the exercise of parental rights by a school or court.

In re (In the matter of)

A method of entitling a judicial proceeding in which there are not adversaries. "In re Batalowme" means in the matter of Batalowme.

Incompetent (Person)

Legal term meaning a person has been declared by law or a judicial officer at a competency hearing to be incapable of exercising some civil right or privilege. Persons can be generally incompetent to make legally important decisions, in which case they are often not held responsible for their acts and not allowed to make critical decisions.

They can also be legally incompetent for only a single civil right or privilege, such as the right to give consent. Legal incompetence is a legal status and not identical to practical or medical incompetence.

Incorrigibility
Term used in describing a sociopath or psychopath that could not be rehabilitated by correctional programs and facilities.

Incriminate
To involve in a crime, to cause to appear guilty.

Independent Contractor
One who agrees to undertake work without being under the direct control or direction of the employer.

Indeterminate Confinement
Keeping someone locked up in a mental institution with no specified time for release. Hospitals formerly locked up mental patients until medical staff members determined they were cured. In most jurisdictions indeterminate confinement is not legal unless it is a result of a judicial proceeding.

Indictment
Formal written accusation, found and presented by a grand jury or a judge, charging a person therein named with criminal conduct.

In-Fact Causation
That which directly caused another. An incident that can be linked directly, immediately, and factually to another event. If "A" caused "B" without any intervening variable, A is the cause "in-fact."

Infliction of Emotional Distress
When the defendant is not an expert this is an intentional tort cause of action. The offender must intend to cause emotional distress to the victim and succeed, and the conduct must be such that an ordinary reasonable citizen would exclaim "outrageous!" on hearing of it. If the conduct is by an expert, the tort is a negligence tort and only professional negligence, instead only intentionality, must be proved. See *Negligent Infliction of Emotional Distress* See *Intentional Infliction of Emotional Distress.*

Informed Consent
A client's right to agree to participate in counseling, assessment, or professional procedures or services after such services are fully described and explained in a manner that is comprehensible to the client. A legal concept that provides that a patient has the right to know the potential risks, benefits, and alternatives of a proposed procedure prior to undergoing a course of therapy. This should be done before commencement of treatment (except in emergency or crisis situations) and should be repeated before any substantial change in treatment is undertaken.

Injunction
A court order prohibiting a person from committing an act that

threatens or may result in injury to another or to the plaintiff.

Innovative Therapy

Therapy or therapeutic techniques and procedures that are unique, being newly-trialed, experimental, contemporary or different from what is traditionally done by the profession.

In-Patient

The status of being treated in a residential setting such as a mental hospital. Therapists have more duties to control inpatients. The opposite is out-patient – a status which allows a client to go home after receiving treatment from a facility.

Inquest

An inquiry made by a coroner to determine the cause of death of someone who has died under circumstances requiring such investigation (e.g., under suspicious circumstances or in prison).

Insanity

A legal status achieved by convincing a trier-of-fact that a defendant is not capable of being responsible for his or her criminal behavior. Sometimes used to describe a medical condition similar to serious mental illness. See *Insanity Defense*.

Insanity Defense

Defense which asserts that defendant's action is a result of his or her mental dysfunctionality. There are four versions of insanity defense.

- **Durham Test.** To establish a defense on the grounds of insanity under this test, defendant's lawyer must clearly prove that at the time of the crime, defendant's mental disease made it impossible for him to know the nature and quality of the act he was committing. Defendant did not know he/she was doing what was wrong and the act is a product of his mental dysfunctionality.

- **Model Penal Code Test.** To establish a defense of insanity under this test, it must be clearly shown that as a result of mental disease or defect, defendant substantially lacked the capacity to appreciate the criminality or wrongfulness of his her conduct or to conform to the requirements of law.

- **M'Naghten Test.** To establish a defense of insanity under this test, it must be clearly shown that because of his/her mental disease or defect, defendant was incapable of forming the guilty intent or mind set required by the crime.

- **Irresistible Impulse Test.** To establish a defense of insanity under this test, it must be clearly shown that defendant had a mental disease and that his or her action is an irresistible result of his/her mental disease.

Institutionalization
Placing a person in a mental institution. If it is against that person's will, it is called "involuntary confinement."

Institutionalization Review Board (IRB)
A human subjects (participants) committee that services an entire institution. The board should include a community representative and be diverse in membership. IRBs are required by federal law for all organizations whose research is supported by federal funds. See *Human Subjects Committee.*

Intent
A state of mind in which the person knows and desires the consequences of his or her act. Legal intent does not require that defendant know or desire the magnitude of damage caused by his or her action. In most cases of criminal liability, intent must exist at the time the offense is committed. Intent is generally not necessary for civil findings of negligence.

Intentional Tort
A tort requiring "willful and malicious" motives or sometimes reckless disregard of the consequences of an act. See *Tort.*

Interrogatories
List of questions sent from one party in a lawsuit to the other party to be answered under oath. See *Discovery.*

Intuitive Level
A level of decision making which provides a forum to allow the richness and influence of everyday personal, professional and moral wisdom to be incorporated into the individual professional's process of ethical decision-making.

Invasion of Privacy
A tort cause of action for the disclosure of a true but private and damaging facts about another. This is an intentional tort.

Invitee
A person who is on the property of another by expressed invitation. Clients are usually considered business invitees and are owed a high duty of protection from environmental harm.

Involuntary Confinement
Placing a person in a mental institution or keeping a person locked up against his or her will. Without clinical justification and/or legal due process, this is actionable under false imprisonment as a tort.

Irreconcilable Differences
Differences that cannot be mended in a marriage. No-Fault grounds for divorce. *Other Names, Irremediable Breakup,* Irreconcilable Breakdown.

Irresistible Impulse Test
See *Insanity Defense.*

J

Joint Commission of Accredidation of Healthcare Org. (JCAHO)

A not-for-profit independent organization dedicated to improving the quality of health care in organized health care setting. The major functions of the JCAHO include development of organizational standards, awarding accreditation decisions, and providing education and consultation to health care organizations.

Joint Custody

Shared custody; A custody arrangement where each parent has significant time with the children and each parent shares in significant decisions. Combined joint legal and physical custody.

Joint Legal Custody

Shared rights to make important decisions about children including medical, religious, and educational decisions.

Joint Physical Custody

Each parent has significant time living with the child. In California the joint custody parent with less time must have at least 135 days living with the child.

Judgment

A decision rendered by a court.

Judgment on the Merits

A decision or judgment based on the essential facts of the case rather than on a technical rule. A decision on the merits is rendered by the trier-of-fact (a jury, or in cases with no jury, the judge).

Judicial Notice

A shortcut for the admission of common knowledge during a trial. The judge's official on-the-record notice of the undisputed fact which admits the fact into evidence.

Judicial Officer

An officer of the court empowered to make legal decisions. Usually a judge or judicial commissioner although in some situations a layperson or an attorney, sitting as a judge pro tem (temporary judge).

Judicial Review

The power of a court to declare a statute unconstitutional. The process and power to interpret the meaning of laws.

Jurisdiction

A court's authority to hear a case or the geographical area within which a court has the right and power to operate. Original jurisdiction means that the court will be the first to hear the case; appellate jurisdiction means that the court reviews cases on appeal from lower court rulings on the subject matter or in a geographical area.

Jurisprudence

Philosophy or science of law on which a particular legal system is built, e.g., American jurisprudence refers to the totality of American law and legal system.

Jury

Certain number of persons selected and sworn in to hear the evidence and determine the facts in a case.

Jury Instructions

Instructions read by a judge or court clerk to a jury that define the questions that the jury must resolve and the legal rules to be applied in answering those questions. Lawyers often request special jury instructions thought to favor their client's position.

Justice

The idea of fairness and equality in terms of access to resources and in the way everyone is treated. Equal treatment of all under the law.

K

Knew-or-Should-Have-Known Doctrine

The legal test for responsibility for knowing something. Ignorance of the law is no excuse when you "should have known."

L

Larceny

Taking of another person's property without consent with the intent to permanently deprive the owner of its use and ownership.

Law

Basic rules of order as pronounced by a government. Statutory law refers to laws passed by legislatures and recorded in public documents. Case law or common law refers to the pronouncements of courts.

Law of Evidence

The law that specifies what types of evidence can be admitted during legal proceedings and how and when they are admissible.

Lay Witness

A witness who is not an expert witness. The scope of the testimony of lay witness is usually more restricted than for experts.

Laying on Evidentiary Foundation

The normal procedure for qualifying an item or potential evidence to be admitted as evidence by the judge in a trial. Before most evidence is admitted, the side offering it must provide preliminary facts showing that it is likely to be authentic, relevant, and reliable.

Leading Question

A question asked by a lawyer at trial or deposition that suggests to the witness the answer that he or she should give. Leading questions are allowed when the witness is one who is defined as "hostile" or an adverse witness. Leading questions are used during cross-examination.

Least Restrictive Alternative

The legal doctrine requiring application of the least confining or least harmful treatment or placement. Treatments given in the least restrictive setting are prepared over those given in most restrictive settings all things being equal. Outpatient therapy is less confining than inpatient treatment in a mental hospital.

Legal Conclusion
A conclusion of fact related to the determination to be made by the trier-of-fact in a verdict. For example: the defendant is guilty.

Legal Duty
In tort law a duty imposed by case law or a statute. If a person having the duty breaches it, he or she may be liable for damages.

Legal Guardian
A person who is appointed by a court to make decisions regarding the overall welfare of another person.

Legal Model
The theoretical model of ideal professional behaviors for attorneys. Core values include using logic and authority to identify truth, and practicing advocacy, loyalty to clients, and solving complex conflicts by applying logic and legal precedent.

Legal Notice
Legally sufficient notice of a pending legal action (such as a lawsuit). Often called "notice." See *Service of Process*.

Legal Representative
An adult empowered or authorized by a court to make legal decisions for a minor or an incompetent adult.

Legal Test
A question relating to legal condition (such as legal insanity). The question may have multiple propositions, usually read to a jury. If the jury decides that the facts of a case allow them to answer yes to the propositions, the test will be passed. For example, if a jury decides that the facts of a case allow them to answer yes to the test for legal insanity, then they must give a verdict of not guilty by reason of insanity.

Legal Wrong
Invasion of a protect right. Behavior or an act that violates a law. Defamation and breach of confidentiality are examples of legal wrongs.

Level of Reasonable Certainty
The clear and convincing evidence level of a burden of proof that is applied to certain cases such as age discrimination, sex discrimination, and mental health cases. See *Burden of Proof*.

Liability
An obligation one has incurred or might incur through a negligent act. A legal responsibility in civil cases, similar to guilt in criminal cases

Liability Insurance
Contract to have someone else pay for any liability or loss that might result from negligence in return for the payment of premiums. It is illegal and against public policy to buy or sell insurance for criminal acts e.g., murder.

Liable
Bound or obligated by law; responsible for actions that may involve restitution.

Libel
False or malicious writing that is intended to defame or dishonor another person and is published so

that someone other than the one defamed will observe it. Writing that injures a person's reputation.

Licensing Board
A government agency empowered to regulate testing and other qualifications for a professional license as well as the conduct of professionals having that license.

Licensing Exam
An examination given or approved by a licensing board that must be passed to obtain a license to practice a regulated profession.

Licensing Statute
A law that specifies the requirements for professional licensing and that regulates the conduct of persons licensed under the law.

Licensure
A type of professional regulation that restricts both the use of a professional title, such as "counselor," and/or the practice of the profession.

Litigation
A legal battle fought in a courtroom; the adversary legal process. The formal contesting of dispute in a court, a lawsuit. The opposite of negotiation.

Living Will
Document in which an individual expresses in advance his or her wishes regarding the application of life-sustaining treatment in the event he or she is incapable of doing so at some future time.

Locality Rule
The legal principle that evaluates the practice and negligence of a professional based only on the manner and methods of practice that is used by a majority of professionals in the particular geographical area in which the professional practices. Locality Rule has mostly given way to national professional standards.

M

M'Naughten Test
The logical test of legal insanity established as a result of the M'Naughten case in Victorian England. Essentially the defendant, by reason of mental disorder, must be incapable of understanding the difference between right and wrong. See *Insanity Defense*.

Majority Opinion
The statement or writing expressing the views of the majority of judges in a court decision.

Malfeasance
Commission of an unlawful act. Execution of an unlawful or improper act.

Malice
The intentional commission of a wrongful act without justification or consideration of its consequences.

Malicious Prosecution
A legal cause of action against defendant alleging that a previous case filed by defendant against

plaintiff was based purely on personal animosity. A tort cause of action requiring that the current plaintiff suing on grounds of malicious prosecution prove that the current defendant's motives for filing the previous legal action were related to personal animosity or other forbidden motives and therefore not legitimate.

Malpractice

A violation of a professional duty or duties expected of a seasonably prudent professional. Performing below the professional due-care standard. Related terms:

- **Malfeasance** is an execution of an unlawful or improper act.
- **Nonfeasance** is failure to act as a reasonably prudent professional would in similar circumstance when there is a duty to act.
- **Misfeasance** is improper performance of an act.

Managed Care

Provision of health services through medical insurance managed or overseen by a contracted company that serves as a mediator between insurance carriers and health professionals.

Managed Care Contract

An agreement between a managed care company and the provider of counseling services; the contract usually defines the type of services that can be provided, the maximum fee, and other limitations to services.

Mandamus

Action brought in a court of competent jurisdiction to compel a lower court or administrative agency to perform or not to perform a specific act or duty.

Mandate

A judicial command, order, or direction.

Mandatory Ethics

The most basic level of ethical guidance focusing on compliance with laws and dictates of professional codes of ethics. Ethical requirements and regulations that are not optional for the practice of that profession.

Mandatory Reporting Law

A law requiring specified people or professional to report specified information to specified government officials. These laws take precedence over laws protecting confidentiality. For example, therapist must report credible evidence of child abuse.

Marital Communications Privilege

The right of a spouse to forbid the other spouse from testifying against him or her in a legal proceeding. In many jurisdictions private communications between spouses during marriage are privileged at the option of a witness spouse. In some states either spouse can prevent the other from testifying about those communications, even after divorce.

Marital Property
Property that belongs to a couple and will be divided at divorce. In a community property states this is also called community property.

Marital Rape
Forced sexual intercourse occurring in a marriage.

Marital Settlement Agreement
An agreement between divorcing parties that settles one or more of the issues that otherwise would be litigated and decided by judicial order after a trail. Often made into an order.

Marriage and Family Therapists
Counselors specializing in marriage and family work. Counselors certified or licensed in marriage and family therapy.

Material
Important, significant, or relevant. Material fact is that which is important, significant or relevant to a case or a legal proceeding. Fact going to the heart of a matter and necessary to reach a decision.

Mayhem
Crime of intentionally disfiguring or dismembering another. Crime of outrageous nature that inflicts serious wounds on the body of another.

Mediation
An alternative dispute resolution process in which the mediator helps the parties arrive at their own solution. Divorce mediation usually is a private mediation of the terms of divorce by a lawyer or a mental health professional or a team composed of both a mental health professional and an attorney.

Medicaid
Medical assistance provided in Title XIX of the Social Security Act. Medicaid is a state-administered program for the medically indigent.

Medicare
Medical assistance provided in Title XVIII of the Social Security Act. Medicare is a health insurance program administered by the Social Security Administration for persons aged 65 years and older and for disabled persons who are eligible for benefits. Medicare Part A benefits provide coverage for inpatient hospital care, skilled nursing facility care, home health care, and hospice care. Medicare Part B benefits provide coverage for physician services, outpatient hospital services, diagnostic test, therapies, durable medical equipment, medical supplies, and prosthetic devices.

Medication (Psychotropic)
Psychoactive drugs used to treat or reduce symptoms of mental illness. A graduate course in psychopharmacology is usually advisable for mental health professionals whose clientele are likely to be on medication.

Medication Error
Any error in the medication process that might occur from the time a medication is ordered until the time it is administered. Wrong

medication, wrong client, wrong dosage, and wrong time are all types medication-related error.

Mens Rea

A guilty mind. The intention or mindset to commit a crime. A necessary element for allegation and conviction of defendant in intentional crimes (e.g. murder).

Mental Anguish (Mental Distress)

A compensable injury covering all forms of mental, as opposed to physical pain (e.g., anxiety, fear, grief). See *Pain and Suffering*.

Mental Health Law

The laws governing the confinement and treatment of mentally ill and mentally retarded persons and characterized by a blend of criminal law-like protections with an intermediate standard (burden) of proof. Law governing and controlling the affairs, processes, program of mental health activities, professionals and institutions.

Mental Health Professionals

Professionals who work in mental health field (counseling, psychology, psychiatry and social work). Professionals whose work, skill and knowledge focus on research, understanding and management of human and other animal behavior.

Mental Hospital

A hospital or institution for the treatment and confinement of the mentally ill. An example is a Psychiatric Center.

Mental Status Examination

A structured interview or process designed to provide a controlled interpersonal setting for the emergence and observation of symptoms and signs of mental disorder.

Mentally Retarded

A term that denotes subnormal intelligence and adaptive abilities. In most of such cases, there may be global deficits in behavior, cognition and affect.

Minority Opinion

A statement or writing expressing the views of a judge or a minority of judges in a court decision. This may take the form of separate opinions by the judges.

Miranda Warning

A warning required to be given by police when an investigation turns accusatorial. The police must warn defendants of the adverse legal consequences of confession or other statements, and inform them of their right to an attorney. Based on *Miranda v Arizona* (1966).

Misdemeanor

An intermediate-level crime, more serious than an infraction (a parking ticket) and less serious than a felony (murder). Normally penalties for being found guilty of a misdemeanor are limited to fines and less than one year in jail.

Misfeasance

Improper performance of a lawful act or duty. This is a type of malpractice.

Misprision of Felony
A misdemeanor now largely limited to concealing a felony that has been committed by oneself or someone else; may rarely apply to failing to take reasonable and safe steps to prevent or disclose a felony (e.g., call the police). Concealment is a major element in this crime.

Misrepresentation (or Deceit)
An intentional tort based on deception which cause harm. A false statement calculated to mislead another.

Mistrial
A trial that is stopped by the judge and declared void prior to a verdict by the fact finder (jury or, in the absence of a jury, judge). It does not result in a judgment for either party, but indicates a failure of the trial process.

Mitigation
The reduction in a fine, penalty, sentence, or damages initially assessed or decreed against a defendant because of a material fact.

Mock Jury
A simulated jury used in research and to test a lawyer's trail strategies. Also called a surrogate jury.

Model Penal Code Test
See *Insanity Defense*.

Modification of Orders
The result of legal procedures to change orders such as custody orders. The change of previous legal orders in accordance with legal guidelines.

Moot Abstract (Case)
Not a real case involving a real dispute. A moot case is that which can no longer be active because the contested issues have materially changed as a result of passage of time or changes resulting from other developments in law or fact.

Moral Certainty
An old term for "beyond a reasonable doubt."

Morality
Judgments as to whether a human act conforms to the accepted rules of righteousness or virtue, which implies the application of religious standards.

Morals
Conduct or behavior related to one's belief structure regarding the nature of right and wrong. Morals, as with morality, imply a religious standard.

Motion
A request made by a lawyer or litigant that a judge take certain action, such as dismissing a case

Motion in Limine
A preliminary motion made for the purpose of limiting or excluding evidence prior to trial.

N

Natural Law
A philosophical concept based on the idea that ideal law exists in nature and can be discovered by armchair induction or by a reasonable person. A concept

advance by the Greek philosopher Aristotle.

Negligence

Failure to exercise ordinary prudence oversight or foresight when a person or professional has a duty to do so. Lack of proper care; failure to exercise prudence which result in injury to another. Omission or commission of an act that a reasonably prudent person or professional would or would not do under given circumstances. It is a form of heedlessness or carelessness that constitutes a departure from the standard of care generally imposed on members of society.

Negligence Per Se

A doctrine in tort law that infers guilt because the legal violation is committed against a member of a class of people a particular law is designed to protect. It is negligence per se for a driver to hit a pedestrian on a pedestrian crossing because "Yield to Pedestrian" signs and laws are designed to protect pedestrians.

Negligent Infliction of Emotional Distress

An unintentional tort or cause of action applied only against negligent professionals and persons. Emotional distress which is a direct or proximate result of a person's negligence. See *Infliction of Emotional Distress.*

Next of Kin

Those persons who by the law of descent would be adjudged the closest blood relatives of the decedent. The person designated by a decedent to inherit or take over his/her assets and liabilities.

No-Fault

In family law this refers to a divorce based on relationship incompatibilities instead of the wrongdoing of a partner. No-fault grounds may include irreconcilable differences instead of adultery and cruelty, as required in fault divorces. Intended to reduce prolong litigation and the bitterness of divorce the no-fault doctrine advocates avoiding determining fault   See *Fault Doctrine.*

Nolens Volens

Whether willing or unwilling. Legal compliance rules that are not voluntary.

Nolo Contendere

A statement that a defendant will not contest a charge made by the government. The statement (not really a plea) is often made to resolve a criminal situation, and may be used to avoid civil effects of criminal sanctions.

Noncustodial Parent

The divorced parent who has less than one third of a year with the children and who is usually ordered to pay child support. The parent who has only visitation rights to see the child and the obligation to pay child support.

Nonfeasance

Failure to act, when there is a duty to do so in a manner required of a reasonably prudent person in similar circumstances. For a professional, this is a kind of malpractice.

Nonsuit

A judgment rendered against a plaintiff who fails to proceed to trial or is unable to prove his or her case. It does not decide the merits of the case, and thus does not preclude the plaintiff's bringing the suit again.

Normalization

A rehabilitation principle that dictates that persons with disabilities should be treated in a manner that allows them to participate both symbolically and actually in roles and lifestyles that are normal for a person of their age, culture and social context.

Norms

Collections of data from large-scale administrations of a test that show how well different types of research participants do on the test. Normative distributions are used for comparisons of a present client's score against other person's scores from particular populations.

Not Guilty By Reason of Insanity (NGI)

A finding that a defendant should not be held responsible for criminal acts because the defendant is legally insane, (as defined by a legal test) at the time he or she committed the criminal acts. See *Insanity Defense*.

Nuisance

A condition that restricts the use of property or creates a potentially dangerous and/or offensive situation for the user.

Nuncupative Will

Oral statement intended as a last will made in anticipation of death of the person who made the statement.

Nuremberg Code

Ten legal principles found in the *U.S. v Karl Brandt* in which the judge outlined basic moral, ethical and legal concepts that should govern human subject research. The code embodies the following principles:

- Legal capacity to give consent
- Situation that does not inhibit the exercise of free will
- Absence of any element of force
- Absence of fraud
- Absence of deceit
- Absence of duress
- Absence of control
- Absence of constraint
- Absence of coercion
- Presence of sufficient knowledge and comprehension of the research issues to enable subject to make an enlightened decision.

O

Objection

An attempt by an attorney to prevent evidence from being admitted during a trial based on allegations that the evidence does not fit the rules of evidence.

Ombudsperson (Ombudsman)

Person who is designated usually by an agency, to speak or act on behalf of a patient/resident, especially in regard to his or her daily needs or conflict with the agency. Conflict resolution point-person in any organization.

On-Line Counseling

Counseling on the internet. This remains controversial as a result of many professional problems with confidentiality, consent, counselor-client relationship etc.

Opinion

A judge's statement of the decision reached in a case. In a case decided by more than one judge, which also results in different opinions, these related terms may be used to characterize the opinions. Related terms:

- **Concurring Opinion** Agrees with the majority opinion but gives different or added reasons for arriving at that opinion.
- **Dissenting Opinion** Disagrees with the majority opinion.
- **Majority Opinion** The opinion agreed on by more than half of the judges or justices hearing a case,

sometimes called the opinion of the court.

- **Minority Opinion** The opinion of fewer than half of the judges or justices hearing a case

Opinion of the Court

In an appellate court decision, the reasons for the decision. One judge writes the opinion for the majority of the court. Judges who agree with the result, but for different reasons, may write concurring opinions explaining their reasons. Judges who disagree with the majority may write dissenting opinions. See *Opinion.*

Order to Show Cause (OSC)

A type of pretrial hearing at which both parties can be present. Court proceeding used to decide temporary support, custody, and measures for prevention of abuse.

Ordinance

A municipal legislative enactment. Law passed by a municipal legislative body.

Original Jurisdiction

The jurisdiction of a court to entertain or hear a case at the inception of that case, as contrasted with appellate jurisdiction which referred to the authority a court has to hear appeals.

Outpatient

The status of being a patient not living in a residential treatment facility.

P

Pain and Suffering
A kind of damages that a person may recover for physical or mental discomfort that results from a legal wrong done against him or her.

Palliative Care
Care that is intended to keep a person comfortable but not intended to prolong life. Lack of provision of palliative due care can lead to the assertion of negligent infliction of emotional distress by a close family member who lived through and experienced the suffering of their loved one. For example, a husband who was going to die any way, but whose dying process was made outrageously uncomfortable by negligent withdrawal of pain relieving medication.

Parens Patriae
The power of a government to act as the parent of a person for the person's own good or protection. The legal doctrine that the state has the right to act as parent to those unable to properly protect their own interests such as children and disabled or disturbed individuals. The state as a sovereign caregiver and protector. Referring to the sovereign power of guardianship over persons such as minors.

Parental Alienation Syndrome (PAS)
The condition of children becoming alienated from one parent, usually the noncustodial parent; often the result of manipulation by the custodial parent.

Parental Kidnapping
The stealing of a child by his or her own parent in violation of a court order. It is a federal crime as well as a state crime in most states. Counselors who aid a parent in anyway in this violation may be found guilty of accessory to a crime (before, during, or after the crime).

Parental Rights
Rights to support and be supported by a child; rights to legally claim a child and to make decisions for the child.

Parole
A conditional release from prison. Letting a person out of prison before the time stated in the sentence usually because of good behavior or poor physical or mental health. The parolee may or may not be returned to prison after the expiration of a condition.

Paternity Suit
A lawsuit to establish fatherhood. Once established, fatherhood usually means duties of paying support and rights of visitation.

Patient (Client)
One with whom a therapist forms a therapeutic relationship for the purpose of clinical evaluation, diagnosis, treatment, or care. A therapeutic relationship is present between clinician and patient even if the patient is called something else (e.g., confidant), so long as the

purpose of the relationship is the same.

Peer Review
A process by which a group of mental health professionals voluntarily participate in group discussions, evaluations and review of their work for the purpose of professional growth and development.

Peer Review Organization (PRO)
Organization that has a contract with the Health Care Financing Administration (HCFA) to review, under part B of Title XI of the Social Security Act, the health care services or items furnished or proposed to be furnished to Medicare beneficiaries.

Per Curiam
An opinion rendered by an entire court, as opposed to an opinion of any one of several justices.

Performance Improvement Plan
A written plan that describes the design for a systematic and ongoing process for monitoring and evaluating patient care. The process for identifying high-risk areas having the potential for adverse outcomes and increased exposure to litigation; and the methodology for identifying opportunities for improvement.

Perjury
Willful act of giving false testimony under oath in a material matter or issue.

Personal Counseling
Counseling that involves professional helpers who assist clients to understand, accept, and resolve their problems by using basic counseling techniques so that their clients can lead more satisfying, well adjusted lives.

Petition
A written application to a court for the redress of a wrong, the grant of a privilege or a license.

Petitioner
One who initiates a legal action or proceeding and requests that some relief be granted on his or her behalf. A person who files for divorce is a petitioner or plaintiff. When the term petitioner is used, the one against whom the petitioner is complaining is referred to as the respondent.

Physical Evidence
Material things introduced into evidence including fingerprints. Usually refers to evidence than can be see, touched, smell, heard, or tasted.

Physical Therapy
Art and science of preventing and treating neuromuscular or musculoskeletal disabilities with physical agents as heat and cold, electricity, water, light, and neuromuscular procedures that, through their physiological effect, improve or maintain the patient's optimum functional level.

Plagiarism
The act of stealing or passing off the ideas, works, or words of another author or person as one's own original work.

Plaintiff
Party who brings a civil suit or who filed the initial papers in a lawsuit. The suing party or the party who brings action by filing a complaint. Called the petitioner in no-fault divorce actions. See *Petitioner*.

Plea
A formal allegation filed by a defendant in an action in reply to the plaintiff's complaint or charges.

Pleadings
Formal documents filed in a court action. They include the plaintiff's complaint and the defendant's reply indicating that which is alleged by one party and denied or conceded by the other party.

Plenary
Full, entire, complete. Plenary power means full or complete authority; not needing any other to act or decide. For example, the President's power to pardon is plenary.

Police Power
The power given to governments by the U.S. Constitution that allows them to regulate the public safety and welfare of citizens. The inherent power of the government to impose restrictions to protect the health, safety, and welfare of its citizens.

Political Question
A question that the courts will not decide because it concerns a decision more properly made by another branch of government such as the legislature.

Polygraph
An instrument that simultaneously records several types of physiological responses to questions. Popularly called a lie detector. Generally deemed inadmissible as a conclusive legal evidence.

Pornography
Exposure of private body part of humans. Usually illegal if performed on legally restricted area, places, time or population like minors. Use of pornography in therapy is controversial and may be illegal, unethical or unprofessional.

Posttraumatic Stress Disorder (PTSD)
A pathological condition caused by severe stress, such as experiencing a fire or an earthquake or being divorced. Characterized by an acute stage in which denial, shock, and defensive reaction are dominant and by a chronic stage in which active survival-oriented behaviors and cognitive distortions and restructuring are dominant.

Precedent
Authoritative court decisions addressing identical or similar questions of law. Previous court decision that must be relied upon by a court faced with a case with identical facts. A published appeals court decision that controls or influences the decisions of other courts.

Predicting Dangerousness (of a client)

The act of determining which client will hurt someone else or attempt suicide or self injury. A duty placed by the judicial community on mental health professionals to determine which of their clients will foreseeably cause harm to self and/or other. Ability to always predict dangerousness with accuracy, remains illusive for most mental health professionals.

Predictive Validity

The extent to which a test predicts relevant real-world behaviors. A form of criterion-referenced validity.

Preferred Provider Organization (PPO)

A health care financing partnership between provider and payer where services are prepaid by periodic fees to the PPO and services are provided by a network of approved health care professional who usually agree to accept fixed fees from the managing organization for different procedures.

Preliminary Hearing

In criminal law, a means of determining whether or not a probably cause for an arrest existed. A hearing held to determine if an indictment is warranted.

Premeditation (and deliberation)

A measure of intentionality use in criminal cases. The act of forethought and/or thoughtful planning and preparation that precedes a crime.

Prenuptial Agreement

See *Antenuptial Agreement.*

Prima Facie

At first view; that which looks to be the fact at first glance. A fact presumed to be true if not rebutted or proven untrue. A set of facts that will win a case (if not rebutted) because they meet predetermined legal criteria.

Privacy

A client's right to keep everything about the counseling relationship a secret. Privacy is more inclusive than confidentiality in which addresses communication in the counseling context.

Privilege

A legal right to refuse to cooperate with a legal request for information (usually a subpoena) about confidential disclosures. There are specialized privileges for different classes of professionals and their clients that differ from state to state. The attorney-client, physician-patient, and pastor-patient privileges are examples. The U.S. Supreme Court created a universal psychotherapist-client privilege in *Jeffe v. Redmond*.

Privileged Communication

A client's right by which he or she can prevent a therapist from revealing confidential information in a legal proceeding (e.g., a legal hearing or court room). Exception to this rule is when the law requires that a therapist report an illegal activity, e.g. child abuse.

Pro Bono

Providing a service for no fee to those in need.

Pro Se

In person, in their own behalf. Representing one's self in a legal proceeding.

Probate Law

The laws governing the settling of wills and the treatment of legally incompetent persons who do not qualify for treatment as mentally ill. It is essentially the law of civil competency.

Procedural Law

The laws regulating legal procedures for litigation for all types of substantive law. Examples of procedural laws are the rules specifying how a plaintiff must have papers served on a defendant and the permissible types of discovery. The law of criminal procedure governs how criminals are prosecuted.

Product Liability

A tort or cause of action making manufactures and sellers of defective or unreasonably dangerous products, liable for injuries those products caused to buyers, users, and bystanders.

Professional Malpractice

A lawsuit brought against a professional, usually alleging that the defendant breached the professional duty of care owed to a plaintiff client.

Professional Sanctions

A punishment delivered by a professional board or association to one of its members. If the person accused refuses to cooperate, the likely penalty is expulsion of that person from membership.

Prognosis

Informed judgment regarding the likely course and probable outcome of a disease or disfunctionality.

Property Settlement

A process of division of property at divorce. In the community property states it is usually an even division of property acquired during marriage. In most other states all property is supposed to be divided on the basis of fairness and equity.

Proprietary Function

Those functions not normally required by statues or law. Functions as it relates to property, usually involving a state or government agent. Functioning as an owner of something. Clients have proprietary authority over their counseling file and information while counselors have fiduciary and professional authority and responsibility over the same documents.

Protective Order

An order granted to an abused person telling the abuser to stay away from a residence or from other places and to stop the harassment or stalking. Violations are punishable by contempt of court.

Protective Service

A government agency charged with protecting children from physical, sexual, and emotional abuse. It has quasi-police powers and can remove children from homes. In most states abuse is reported to these agencies. Professionals who work in child protective services have limited immunity.

Protocol

A set of rules governing a required process or procedure.

Proximate Cause

Legal cause. That deemed by the law to be a reason why something happened. In immediate relation with what happened. Related term: *Cause "in-fact" or direct cause*

Psychological Miranda Warning

A therapist's pre-therapy warning to a client about exceptions to confidentiality. See *Informed Consent.*

Psychological Testimony

The expert testimony of a mental health professional usually about a mental health condition, program, process, progress or prognosis.

Psychological Testing

The measurement of cognitive, behavioral and affective variables using psychometric instruments. Licensure laws and some case laws in many states specify what training and experience are needed for different types of psychological testing. Professionals should ensure the practices within those guidelines or get the required training.

Psychometrics

Having to do with the measurement of psychological variables, usually using psychological tests. The science of test design and use.

Psychotropic Medication

Those medications used in the treatment and/or management of psychological conditions. Medications that have the capability of altering cognition, mood and behavior.

Punitive Damages

The damages awarded only to successful plaintiffs in intentional tort lawsuits and designed to punish or hurt defendants who have committed outrageous acts.

Putative Spouse

An innocent person who thinks he or she is married but who is not legally married. Most states give marital rights to putative spouses.

Q

Qualified Expert

An expert who has been approved to testify by a judge at a trial. An expert is qualified when an attorney provides foundational facts necessary for the expert to be allowed to testify. This is usually done during a "Voir Dire" examination of the expert (See "Voir Dire") and before the case in chief.

Quasi

As if. Almost as it were, analogous to.

Quasi-judicial
The case-deciding function of an administrative agency. Proceedings that follow legal procedures for the resolution of administrative conflicts and problems.

Quid Pro Quo
A consideration given for something of value. Giving one valuable thing in exchange for another.

Quo Warranto
A suit brought to determine whether an officer has the right and authority to exercise the duties of his or her office. An extraordinary proceeding intended to prevent exercise of unlawful power and to inquire "by what authority" one supports a claim to a position or power.

R

Reasonable Care
That level of care that is expected of a professional or person in the execution of his or her duty. A level of care below which reasonable people and professionals will object.

Reasonable Certainty (reasonable |medical, psychological, psychiatric, professional| certainty)
Identical to clear and convincing evidence. Defined differently in different jurisdictions, and sometimes differently for criminal and civil cases (with more certainty for criminal matters); often not defined in most statutes at all. Should not be confused with the certainty necessary to make a diagnosis or to choose a particular treatment.

Rebuttal
Giving of evidence to contradict the effect of evidence previously introduced by the opposing party.

Reckless Disregard
Describes an act or conduct that was committed without concern for the consequences, especially heedless of danger; often "wanton disregard" or "deliberate indifference" to consequences. It implies a defendant's consciousness of a danger and a willingness to assume the risk posed by the danger. When reckless disregard (or "deliberate indifference") occurs with negligence, the level of negligence is often increased (e.g., to "gross negligence"). It does not necessarily require criminal intent to harm.

Redress
To set right, remedy, make up for, remove the cause of a complaint or grievance.

Referral
Informing a client or person with needs of the availability of other professionals or programs that can meet these needs and seeking the client's voluntary transfer to any of those professionals or programs.

Referral Fee

A fee paid by one professional to another for referring a client. Often legal for lawyers but may not be ethical for most mental health professionals because they carry the risk of encouraging referrals not best suited for clients.

Regulation

An administrative rule written by bureaucracies to clarify and explain laws passed by legislatures related to the mandate and mission of the agency. Although not passed by the legislature violation of these executive-branch rules, can carry legal sanctions.

Relationship Advocate (mediator)

A mental health or legal professional who tries to help a particular relationship or relationship process, such as the negotiation of a divorce settlement. The professional does not represent the interests of any one party but instead is an advocate for a solution. See *Divorce Mediation*.

Release

Statement signed by one person relinquishing a right or claim against another. A release protects the defendant from future legal proceeding based on the same facts and issues.

Reliability

The consistency of results across different testing sessions or raters.

Relief

Legal redress or assistance sought in court by the complainant. That which a court grants a plaintiff in response to a request or pleading.

Remand

Referral of a case by an appeals court back to the original court, out of which it came, for the purpose of having some action taken there.

Remedy

A court's enforcement of a right or the prevention of the violation of a right. The means a court employs to enforce a right or redress an injury. Any remedial right to which an aggrieved party is entitled.

Repressed Memories

Objectionable impulses, memories, affects and ideas unconsciously excluded from consciousness but can be excavated on a later time during psychotherapy. Psychological materials pushed under or hidden at the subconscious "mind" because of the pain they cause at the conscious level. Examples are feelings and experiences of childhood sexual abuse.

Res Ipsa Loquitur

"The thing speaks for itself." A doctrine of law applicable to cases where the defendant had exclusive control over the thing that caused the harm and where the harm ordinarily could not have occurred without negligent conduct

Res Judicate

"The thing is decided" – that which has been acted on or decided by the courts. A doctrine of law that seeks to avoid re-litigation of cases thus giving finality to already decided cases. One exception is that a civil action can be brought against a defendant on the basis of the same facts on which a criminal case was based, litigated, and decided.

Respondent

The party against whom an appeal is taken in a higher court. A defendant in an appeal. In family law or divorce case, person who is served with the petitioner's petition requesting divorce in a no-fault divorce state or some other family law action in many states. The respondent may contest the terms of a divorce by filing a response to the petition.

Respondent Superior

"Let the master answer." A aphorism meaning that the employer is responsible for the legal consequences of the acts of the servant or employee who is acting within the scope of his or her employment.

Respondent Superior Doctrine

A principle of law that holds a supervisor or employer responsible for the negligent acts of subordinates. See *Vicarious Liability*. This principle assumes that the superior has control and directs the action of a subordinate. This is the legal doctrine by which clinical supervisors are held liable for the action of supervisors.

Restrain

To enjoin or prohibit; as in restraining order used by a court to avoid potential harmful or offensive interpersonal contact.

Restraining Order

An order forbidding certain private conduct, issued by a court usually at the request of an abused or harassed person. It can be a temporary order granted at an emergency hearing that puts limits on the conduct of another person (such as an ex-spouse). This order is usually good until a second hearing, when everyone can appear and tell their stories. Generally, actions on the part of the beneficiary which permits the abuser to violate the terms of the order, could negate and/or invalidate the order. For example, Mary permits her abusive husband to move back to the house contrary to restraining order.

Restraint

Removing or restricting a person's voluntary movement or choice to act. Restraints can be "physical" or "chemical." A physical restraint involves a device (e.g. safety belts, safety bars, geriatric chairs, and bed rails) that restricts or limits voluntary movement and cannot be removed by the patient. Chemical restraint involves the use of medication or a chemical to immobilize a person. Physical restraint is usually legally permissible when a person is clearly a danger to self or others.

Reversible Error

An error of law during a trial that substantially affects the legal rights of the person who lost, and that, if uncorrected, would result in a miscarriage of justice. An appellate court may reverse a lower court decision based on reversible error, but not on harmless error. See *Harmless Error*.

Revocation (of a professional license)
Refers to the loss of the right to practice in the licensing jurisdiction. Withdrawal of practicing privileges by a government licensing agency usually as a result of professional misconduct.

Right to Decline Medication/Treatment
A constitutionally based right of individuals to refuse medication and/or any treatment. To exercise this right the client or patient must be competent. The best practice is to have the client sign a document to show the knowing and voluntary decline of treatment after consequences of such decline has been explained.

S

Scapegoating
A process whereby one member of a group is placed in an 'odd person out' position or is treated by others as deviant, thereby receiving negative messages from other members of the group.

Scientific Model
The theoretical model of ideal professional behaviors for social and other scientists. A model of investigation and learning that focuses on objective facts and their verifiable relationships; core values include objectivity, empiricism, and logical increasing of knowledge.

Scope of Practice
The extent and limits of activities considered acceptable professional practice by an individual licensed or certified in a profession; a recognized area of proficiency, competence, or skills gained through appropriate education and experience.

Self-Referral
A person who requests mental health or counseling services on his or her own behalf without a referral by another. A minor who goes for counseling without an adult competent to give legal consent for the requested treatment. As a matter of public policy, many states allow counselors to treat minors without parental consent in specified circumstances, such as substance abuse.

Separate Property
In community property states, this refers to property that is not owned together or acquired during marriage. Also means property owned prior to marriage and earning from such property or property acquired by gift or inheritance.

Separation Anxiety Disorder
Pathological symptoms shown by children cut off from contact with one or both parents. This is usually marked by loneliness, fear, and depression.

Service of Process
The delivery of legal notice in a legally acceptable way. Service of complaint on a defendant by a court that has jurisdiction to hear the case. Service usually requires a third party to deliver the papers or by mail and/or publication or other means deemed effective in making defendant aware of his or her duty to defend a law suit.

Settlement
The conclusive resolution of a legal matter. In civil suits, a compromise achieved before litigation or final judgment that eliminates the necessity of a judicial resolution.

Sex Offenders
A person who commits a sexual act that is prohibited by law.

Sex With Clients
A major ethical and/or legal violation in the mental health professions. It is illegal and unethical because it destroys the boundary of the therapeutic relationship and seriously compromises clinical objectivity.

Sexual Abuse (Child)
A form of child abuse involving any type of sexual conduct directed at a minor by an adult or in some cases an older minor.

Sexual Harassment
Persistent and unwanted sexual advances or sexually related activities. Usually from a senior and more dominant person in a workplace or academic setting directed at a junior and weaker person. Always unethical and illegal.

Slander
False oral statement, made in the presence of a third person, that injures the character or reputation of another. See *Defamation*.

Social Constructivism
A philosophical framework that proposes that reality is a creation of individuals in interaction – a socially consensual definition of what is real. An ideology that presumes that change is unavoidable in social realities, relationships, and activities.

Sole Custody
To have the right to make decisions and to have physical custody of a child; therefore being the custodial parent with the right to receive support on behalf of the child. Being a sole custodian does not mean having sole responsibility. Sole custodians usually receive child support.

Sole Proprietorship
A pattern of organizing a business in which one person is the owner and operator of the business. Another pattern common to mental health agencies is "partnership" where two or more persons establish an agency in which all

partners are usually deemed by law to be accountable for any judgments against the agency.

Sovereign Immunity

A doctrine providing that governmental body is immune to suit without the expressed consent or permission of the body itself.

Special Damages

Damages that are unique to a case, and is added as a result of the nature of a particular case. Damages that are not usually for a case of a particular nature.

Spousal Abuse

Domestic Violence directed from one spouse to the other.

Standard of Care

Description of the conduct that is expected of an individual or a professional in a given situation. It is a measure against which a defendant's professional conduct is compared.

Standing

A person's right to bring a lawsuit because he or she is directly affected by the issues raised. The right to raise an issue in a lawsuit.

Stare Decisis

"Let the decision stand." A legal rule requiring that when a court has decided a case by applying a legal principle to a set of facts, that court should stick by that principle and apply it to all later cases with clearly similar facts unless there is a good reason not to. A legal doctrine that prescribes adherence to those precedents set forth in cases that have been decided. This rule promotes fairness and reliability in judicial decision making and is inherent in the American legal system.

Status Quo

The existing state of affairs. The way things are and have been.

Statute

A law or an act passed by the legislative branch of government. Because statutes are always in print form they are also often called black letter laws.

Statute of Limitation

A statute that sets forth the time period within which litigation may be commenced in a particular cause of action. Legal time limit allowed for filing suit in civil matters, usually measured from the time of the wrong or from the time when a reasonable person would have discovered the wrong.

Statutory Law

Law that is prescribed by legislative enactments.

Stay Away Order

A protective order for a batterer, abuser or stalker to remain a specified distance from the home and work place of the person obtaining the order. Also known as restraining order.

Stipulation

Agreement, usually in writing , by attorneys on opposite sides of an issue concerning any matter pertaining to the proceedings. A stipulation is not binding unless agreed on by the parties involved in the issue.

Strict Liability

A legal theory that anyone creating a condition of extreme hazard should be liable for the harm caused by that hazard and the normal requirement that the injured plaintiff prove negligence or bad intentions should be waived. Liability that is imposed just because the harmful act was done.

Subpoena

A court order requesting a person to appear in a legal hearing with all requested information. A court order demanding certain information or the appearance of a certain person.

Subpoena Ad Testificandum

Court order requiring a person to appear in court to give testimony.

Subpoena Duces Tecum

A legal document issued by a court, or an attorney with the approval of a court, that requires the recipient to provide documents and records to the requesting party unless a privilege applies. A subpoena requiring the production of records and usually the appearance of the custodian of those records as part of discovery.

Subrogation

Substitution of one person for another in reference to a lawful claim or right.

Substantive Law

The law that defines, creates, and regulates rights and duties as opposed to procedures for enforcing the rights and duties. Basically every kind of law except procedural law, including family law, contract law, tort law, and criminal law. A combination of established law.

Suggestibility

That which tends to imply culpability or guilt. That said in order to imply a given answer or response.

Suicide

The act of killing oneself and the person who does so. A person at this risk is deemed a danger to self.

Suit

A proceeding in a court of law brought by a plaintiff.

Summary Judgment

A court's decision to settle a dispute or dispose of a case promptly without conducting it full legal proceedings.

Summons

Court order directed to the sheriff or other appropriate official to notify the defendant in a civil suit that a suit has been filed and when and where to appear. A notification to a defendant that a case has been filed against him or her.

Support

The receiving of encouragement, understanding, and kindness from others. Support order is the requirement by a court that one person pays another certain amounts of money (or goods and services) as in child support.

Supreme Court

The highest level of appeals court, which reconciles conflicting decisions of lower appeals courts within that supreme court's jurisdiction. In the United States each state has a supreme court; the U.S. Supreme Court is the highest level of federal court and has jurisdiction over all the state supreme courts.

Surrogate Decision Maker
Individual who has been designated to make decision on behalf of an individual determined incapable of making his or her own decisions. See *Guardian*.

Surrogate Mother
A woman who is hired to be impregnated with the sperm of a man not married to her, to produce a baby for that and (usually) his infertile wife. Also a woman who bears an embryo not her own. Many states forbid the practice.

Suspension (of a license to practice)
A temporary loss of the right to practice a profession within a jurisdiction.

T

Tarasoff Doctrine
The legal duty of a mental health professional to warn or notify identifiable victims of the danger posed to them by any of the professional's clients if such a danger is reasonably foreseeable and imminent. This doctrine is based on *Tarasoff v Regents* of the University of California ruling.

Tarasoff Duty
The duty for mental health professionals created by California courts that is now adopted by most states. The duty is to warn an intended victim of threats made by a client. The duty is an exception to the therapist-client privilege but it is not a mandatory reporting requirement. The penalty for failing to warn an intended victim is a lawsuit by surviving victims or the surviving relatives of non-surviving victims.

Tender years Doctrine
The legal doctrine that custody of young children is best given to mothers because they are seen as primary care givers to children during the early (tender) years of life.

Tenure
An employment security for those who successfully perform duties and meet statutory or contractual requirements of a continuous service contract.

Term of Art
A legal jargon. A word or phrase with a unique meaning in legal writing. For example "malice" means intentional and not hatred in legal texts. Knowing what some terms of art mean helps in understanding case law.

Termination Hearing
In family law (an administrative or court) hearing to decide whether the best interests of a child will be served by severing the ties between the biological parents and the child.

A hearing to consider terminating parental rights.

Testimonial Evidence

The content of testimony by witnesses in court. Oral statement of a witness given as evidence under oath at a trial.

Testing

The use of a test, or a specific tool to gather information or measure some individual quality or characteristic. '

Therapeutic Contract

A client-therapist contract usually outlining intended treatment, payment terms, and exceptions to confidentiality. This becomes effective when the agreement is signed or understanding reached usually during the first session. In crises or emergency situations, it begins when professional contact is made.

Third Party

An individual or organization that is somehow involved with a case (e.g.., referral source) but is not the counselor or the client and not the plaintiff or defendant.

Third Party Rule

The traditional legal rule that when two people have a conversation in the presence of an unrelated third person, there is no expectation of privacy and no confidentiality. The rule affects legal confidentiality in group and family counseling.

Title VII

The section of the Federal Civil Rights Act of 1964 that outlaws gender discrimination including sexual harassment in employment.

Tort

An actionable civil wrong done by one person to another. For an act to be a tort, there must be a legal duty owed by one person to another, a breach of that duty, and harm done as a direct or proximate result of the action. Torts may be classified as intentional or unintentional. If a tort is classified as a criminal wrong (e.g., assault, battery, and false imprisonment), the wrongdoer could be held liable in a criminal action as well as a civil action. See *Negligence and Intentional Tort*.

Tort Law

The civil law of the personal injuries. A civil lawsuit in which an injured party (plaintiff) sues a defendant for money damages. These may involve a contingency fee arrangement under which the attorney is not paid unless the case is successful.

Tort-Feasor

Person who commits a tort.

Trespass

The unauthorized entry upon the property of another; taking or interfering with the property of another.

Trial

The examination of a civil or criminal case by a competent tribunal. It may be made by a judge or judges, with or without a jury.

Trial Court
A court of initial impression that first hears a case. Trial courts apply the existing laws to the facts presented by the litigants and are not allowed to modify those laws. Decisions of trial courts are usually not published and are not precedents.

Tribunal
An officer or body having the authority to adjudicate matters.

Trier of Law
In a trial, the judge, who determines whether or not matters of law have been met and legal processes followed in the trial. When there is no jury, the judge is also the trier of fact as well as "trier of law."

Trier-of-fact
The legal entity that determines and declares which facts are true, usually in the form of a verdict. It may be a jury or a judge sitting in a trial. Its decisions are not precedents. If a litigant is dissatisfied with a verdict from a trier-of-fact they are allowed to appeal to an appeals court.

U

U.S. Supreme Court
The highest court in the federal system of the United States. It reconciles conflicting opinions of the federal circuit courts of appeals and of the state supreme courts. It may also hear cases arising from lower levels of the judicial system and may interpret federal statutes. Its holdings are the law of the land.

Ultra Vires
Going beyond the specifically delegated authority to act. For example, a school president who is by law and jurisdiction not authorized to punish students for behavior occurring wholly off campus, acts "ultra vires" in punishing any student for behavior observed at a private off-campus party. Acting beyond professional authority.

Umbrella Rule (Principle)
A legal concept that permits all professionals who work in a mental health agency to have some access to confidential client information. The rule also imposes confidentiality obligations on all such access. It is the basis on which secretaries and directors of mental health agencies can work with the files whether or not they are trained as psychotherapists.

Undue Influence
Influence put on another that destroys his or her free will or voluntary action. Considered unprofessional, unethical, and/or illegal as it relates to issues of consent or clinical propriety.

Unlawful Detention
A tort or cause of action based on a detention of a person in violation of legally sanctioned procedures. Usually applies in the mental health

professions to situations in which a mental health professional improperly detains an aggressive, suicidal, or agitated client either in his or her office or in a mental health facility. See *False Imprisonment.*

Vacate
To cancel or rescind a court decision.

Values
Personal convictions, beliefs and opinions that shape attitudes and motivate behavior.

Value System
A particular hierarchy or rank-ordering of preference for the values expressed by a particular person or social entity. A collection of social rights and wrongs. A group of social norms that guide human behavior in a given social group.

Venue
Geographic district in which an action or case is or may be brought.

Verdict
Formal declaration of a jury's finding of fact, signed by the jury foreman and presented to the court or judge.

Vicarious Liability
Liability for the acts of others. Usually imposed on employers or supervisors for the acts of their employees or supervisees on the theory that the employer or supervisor violated a direct duty to know what his or her agents were doing and to control the agents' conduct. This liability may be for negligent or intentional acts committed within the scope of that agency's employment activities.

Visitation
The right to have visits at specified times with one's own children; usually granted to non-custodial parents.

Void
Null; without force or a binding effect. Of no effect.

Void Marriage
A marriage that legally never existed. A legally impossible marriage, such as to one's sister.

Voidable Marriage
A marriage that could be annulled at a later time because it was flawed when made, usually by inadequate consent. Grounds for voidable marriage may include fraud, duress, or other illegalities.

Voir Dire
A preliminary questioning of the qualifications and biases of jurors or expert witnesses. The purpose of Voir Dire is the elimination of a juror or witness whose biases might adversely impact on his or her ability to be fair and objective in a legal proceeding.

Voluntariness (in informed consent)
Acting by one's own free will. Acting freely in a decision-making

process. Agreeing to treatment by a person's own free will and without undue influence.

Wage Attachment Action
In family law; a motion or other legal request to a court to order the employer of a defendant who is behind in support payments to deduct the payment from wages in order to pay same to plaintiff through the court.

Waiver
To forego, renounce, or relinquish a legal right. The legal term for a voluntary relinquishment of a known right or the acceptance of a known disadvantage. Waivers allow persons to give up rights either orally, in writing or by behaviors. An example is allowing a counselor to testify to information that ordinarily would be protected as a (client's) privileged communication.

Warrant
A written order of a court that permits a person or agency to do sometime that is ordinarily forbidden by law.

Warranty
A guarantee and a type of contract. A product performance assurance or statement, the failure of which makes the manufacturer or seller

liable for the terms of the agreement.

Will
Legal declaration of the intentions a person wishes to have carried out after their death with regards to anything – property, children, or estate. A will designates a person or persons to serve as the executor(s) responsible for carrying out the instructions of the will.

Witness
One who gives testimony in court under oath. A *fact witness* is one who is allowed to testify on matters that he or she personally knows or has observed. *An expert witness* is one who is allowed to give opinions and to testify in other special ways based on his or her special knowledge or qualification to assist the court in a complex matter. An *adverse* or *hostile witness* is one whose relationship to the opposing party may prejudice his or her testimony. A witness declared to be hostile may be asked leading questions and is subject to cross-examination by the party that called him or her.

Work Product
Usually an attorney's confidential notes and documents related to preparing a case. It may include the work of persons such as therapists hired by the attorney. It is protected by privilege and sometimes applied to other professions. A counselor's journal in which he or she reflects and

strategizes on a case may qualify as a work product.

Worker's Compensation

Payments to disabled workers. Claims for psychological – emotional injuries for the purpose of worker's compensation have increased rapidly, creating employment for mental health experts on both defendants' and claimants' sides.

World View

Values, beliefs, and underlying assumptions a person holds and through which he or she views, interprets, or analyzes people, events, and situations.

Writ

Written order that is issued to a person or persons, requiring the performance of some specified act or giving authority to have it done.

Writ of Mandamus

A command from a court directing a court, officer, or body to perform a certain act.

Wrongful Birth

A cause of action by parents who claim that the negligent advice or treatment deprived them of the choice of aborting or of terminating a pregnancy or that a negligent advice or treatment caused an unwanted pregnancy. Wrongful birth is not actionable in many jurisdictions unless the child is deformed and the deformation is a result (predictably) of the treatment or advice.

Wrongful Commitment

A cause of action brought against a mental health professional for committing a patient to a mental institution in violation of some rule or legal test. A type of unlawful detention. See *Unlawful Detention* and *False Imprisonment*.

Wrongful Death

Preventable or avoidable death caused in-fact or proximately by the negligence or intentional act of another.

Wrongful Life

Refers to a cause of action brought by or on behalf of a defective child who claims that but for the defendant (e.g., a laboratory's negligent testing procedures or a physician's negligent advice or treatment of the child's parents), the child would not have been born or born with the defect.

Appendix A-1
American Counseling Association Code of Ethics

Preamble

The American Counseling Association is an educational, scientific, and professional organization whose members are dedicated to the enhancement of human development throughout the life-span. Association members recognize diversity in our society and embrace a cross-cultural approach in support of the worth, dignity, potential, and uniqueness of each individual.

The specification of a code of ethics enables the association to clarify to current and future members, and to those served by members, the nature of the ethical responsibilities held in common by its members. As the code of ethics of the association, this document establishes principles that define the ethical behavior of association members. All members of the American Counseling Association are required to adhere to the Code of Ethics and the Standards of Practice. The Code of Ethics will serve as the basis for processing ethical complaints initiated against members of the association.

ACA Code of Ethics

> Section A: The Counseling Relationship
> Section B: Confidentiality
> Section C: Professional Responsibility
> Section D: Relationships With Other Professionals
> Section E: Evaluation, Assessment, and Interpretation
> Section F: Teaching, Training, and Supervision
> Section G: Research and Publication
> Section H: Resolving Ethical Issues

Section A: The Counseling Relationship

A.1.   Client Welfare

a. Primary Responsibility. The primary responsibility of counselors is to respect the dignity and to promote the welfare of clients.
b. Positive Growth and Development. Counselors encourage client growth and development in ways that foster the clients + interest and welfare; counselors avoid fostering dependent counseling relationships.

c. Counseling Plans. Counselors and their clients work jointly in devising integrated, individual counseling plans that offer reasonable promise of success and are consistent with abilities and circumstances of clients. Counselors and clients regularly review counseling plans to ensure their continued viability and effectiveness, respecting clients + freedom of choice. (See A.3.b.)

d. Family Involvement. Counselors recognize that families are usually important in clients + lives and strive to enlist family understanding and involvement as a positive resource, when appropriate.

e. Career and Employment Needs. Counselors work with their clients in considering employment in jobs and circumstances that are consistent with the clients + overall abilities, vocational limitations, physical restrictions, general temperament, interest and aptitude patterns, social skills, education, general qualifications, and other relevant characteristics and needs. Counselors neither place nor participate in placing clients in positions that will result in damaging the interest and the welfare of clients, employers, or the public.

A.2.   Respecting Diversity

a. Nondiscrimination. Counselors do not condone or engage in discrimination based on age, color, culture, disability, ethnic group, gender, race, religion, sexual orientation, marital status, or socioeconomic status. (See C.5.a., C.5.b., and D.1.i.)

b. Respecting Differences. Counselors will actively attempt to understand the diverse cultural backgrounds of the clients with whom they work. This includes, but is not limited to, learning how the counselor + s own cultural/ethnic/racial identity impacts her or his values and beliefs about the counseling process. (See E.8. and F.2.i.)

A.3.   Client Rights

a. Disclosure to Clients. When counseling is initiated, and throughout the counseling process as necessary, counselors inform clients of the purposes, goals, techniques, procedures, limitations, potential risks, and benefits of services to be performed, and other pertinent information. Counselors take steps to ensure that clients understand the implications of diagnosis, the intended use of tests and reports, fees, and billing arrangements. Clients have the right to expect confidentiality and to be provided with an explanation of its limitations, including supervision

and/or treatment team professionals; to obtain clear information about
their case records; to participate in the ongoing counseling plans; and to
refuse any recommended services and be advised of the consequences
of such refusal. (See E.5.a. and G.2.)

b.   Freedom of Choice. Counselors offer clients the freedom to choose
whether to enter into a counseling relationship and to determine which
professional(s) will provide counseling. Restrictions that limit choices
of clients are fully explained. (See A.1.c.)

c.   Inability to Give Consent. When counseling minors or persons unable
to give voluntary informed consent, counselors act in these clients +
best interests. (See B.3.)

A.4.   Clients Served by Others

If a client is receiving services from another mental health professional,
counselors, with client consent, inform the professional persons already
involved and develop clear agreements to avoid confusion and conflict
for the client. (See C.6.c.)

A.5.   Personal Needs and Values

a.   Personal Needs. In the counseling relationship, counselors are aware of
the intimacy and responsibilities inherent in the counseling relationship,
maintain respect for clients, and avoid actions that seek to meet their
personal needs at the expense of clients.

b.   Personal Values. Counselors are aware of their own values, attitudes,
beliefs, and behaviors and how these apply in a diverse society, and
avoid imposing their values on clients. (See C.5.a.)

A.6.   Dual Relationships

a.   Avoid When Possible. Counselors are aware of their influential
positions with respect to clients, and they avoid exploiting the trust and
dependency of clients. Counselors make every effort to avoid dual
relationships with clients that could impair professional judgment or
increase the risk of harm to clients. (Examples of such relationships
include, but are not limited to, familial, social, financial, business, or
close personal relationships with clients.) When a dual relationship
cannot be avoided, counselors take appropriate professional precautions
such as informed consent, consultation, supervision, and documentation

to ensure that judgment is not impaired and no exploitation occurs. (See F.1.b.)
b. Superior/Subordinate Relationships. Counselors do not accept as clients superiors or subordinates with whom they have administrative, supervisory, or evaluative relationships.

A.7. Sexual Intimacies With Clients

a. Current Clients. Counselors do not have any type of sexual intimacies with clients and do not counsel persons with whom they have had a sexual relationship.
b. Former Clients. Counselors do not engage in sexual intimacies with former clients within a minimum of 2 years after terminating the counseling relationship. Counselors who engage in such relationship after 2 years following termination have the responsibility to examine and document thoroughly that such relations did not have an exploitative nature, based on factors such as duration of counseling, amount of time since counseling, termination circumstances, client +s personal history and mental status, adverse impact on the client, and actions by the counselor suggesting a plan to initiate a sexual relationship with the client after termination.

A.8. Multiple Clients

When counselors agree to provide counseling services to two or more persons who have a relationship (such as husband and wife, or parents and children), counselors clarify at the outset which person or persons are clients and the nature of the relationships they will have with each involved person. If it becomes apparent that counselors may be called upon to perform potentially conflicting roles, they clarify, adjust, or withdraw from roles appropriately. (See B.2. and B.4.d.)

A.9. Group Work

a. Screening. Counselors screen prospective group counseling/therapy participants. To the extent possible, counselors select members whose needs and goals are compatible with goals of the group, who will not impede the group process, and whose well-being will not be jeopardized by the group experience.
b. Protecting Clients. In a group setting, counselors take reasonable precautions to protect clients from physical or psychological trauma.

A.10.   Fees and Bartering (See D.3.a. and D.3.b.)

a. Advance Understanding. Counselors clearly explain to clients, prior to entering the counseling relationship, all financial arrangements related to professional services including the use of collection agencies or legal measures for nonpayment. (A.11.c.)

b. Establishing Fees. In establishing fees for professional counseling services, counselors consider the financial status of clients and locality. In the event that the established fee structure is inappropriate for a client, assistance is provided in attempting to find comparable services of acceptable cost. (See A.10.d., D.3.a., and D.3.b.)

c. Bartering Discouraged. Counselors ordinarily refrain from accepting goods or services from clients in return for counseling services because such arrangements create inherent potential for conflicts, exploitation, and distortion of the professional relationship. Counselors may participate in bartering only if the relationship is not exploitative, if the client requests it, if a clear written contract is established, and if such arrangements are an accepted practice among professionals in the community. (See A.6.a.)

d. Pro Bono Service. Counselors contribute to society by devoting a portion of their professional activity to services for which there is little or no financial return (pro bono).

A.11.   Termination and Referral

a. Abandonment Prohibited. Counselors do not abandon or neglect clients in counseling. Counselors assist in making appropriate arrangements for the continuation of treatment, when necessary, during interruptions such as vacations, and following termination.

b. Inability to Assist Clients. If counselors determine an inability to be of professional assistance to clients, they avoid entering or immediately terminate a counseling relationship. Counselors are knowledgeable about referral resources and suggest appropriate alternatives. If clients decline the suggested referral, counselors should discontinue the relationship.

c. Appropriate Termination. Counselors terminate a counseling relationship, securing client agreement when possible, when it is reasonably clear that the client is no longer benefiting, when services are no longer required, when counseling no longer serves the client +s needs or interests, when clients do not pay fees charged, or when agency or institution limits do not allow provision of further counseling services. (See A.10.b. and C.2.g.)

A.12.   Computer Technology

a.   Use of Computers. When computer applications are used in counseling services, counselors ensure that (1) the client is intellectually, emotionally, and physically capable of using the computer application; (2) the computer application is appropriate for the needs of the client; (3) the client understands the purpose and operation of the computer applications; and (4) a follow-up of client use of a computer application is provided to correct possible misconceptions, discover inappropriate use, and assess subsequent needs.

b.   Explanation of Limitations. Counselors ensure that clients are provided information as a part of the counseling relationship that adequately explains the limitations of computer technology.

c.   Access to Computer Applications. Counselors provide for equal access to computer applications in counseling services. (See A.2.a.)

Section B: Confidentiality

B.1. Right to Privacy

a.   Respect for Privacy. Counselors respect their clients right to privacy and avoid illegal and unwarranted disclosures of confidential information. (See A.3.a. and B.6.a.)

b.   Client Waiver. The right to privacy may be waived by the client or his or her legally recognized representative.

c.   Exceptions. The general requirement that counselors keep information confidential does not apply when disclosure is required to prevent clear and imminent danger to the client or others or when legal requirements demand that confidential information be revealed. Counselors consult with other professionals when in doubt as to the validity of an exception.

d.   Contagious, Fatal Diseases. A counselor who receives information confirming that a client has a disease commonly known to be both communicable and fatal is justified in disclosing information to an identifiable third party, who by his or her relationship with the client is at a high risk of contracting the disease. Prior to making a disclosure the counselor should ascertain that the client has not already informed the third party about his or her disease and that the client is not intending to inform the third party in the immediate future. (See B.1.c and B.1.f.)

e. Court-Ordered Disclosure. When court ordered to release confidential information without a client +s permission, counselors request to the court that the disclosure not be required due to potential harm to the client or counseling relationship. (See B.1.c.)

f. Minimal Disclosure. When circumstances require the disclosure of confidential information, only essential information is revealed. To the extent possible, clients are informed before confidential information is disclosed.

g. Explanation of Limitations. When counseling is initiated and throughout the counseling process as necessary, counselors inform clients of the limitations of confidentiality and identify foreseeable situations in which confidentiality must be breached. (See G.2.a.)

h. Subordinates. Counselors make every effort to ensure that privacy and confidentiality of clients are maintained by subordinates including employees, supervisees, clerical assistants, and volunteers. (See B.1.a.)

i. Treatment Teams. If client treatment will involve a continued review by a treatment team, the client will be informed of the team+s existence and composition.

B.2. Groups and Families

a. Group Work. In group work, counselors clearly define confidentiality and the parameters for the specific group being entered, explain its importance, and discuss the difficulties related to confidentiality involved in group work. The fact that confidentiality cannot be guaranteed is clearly communicated to group members.

b. Family Counseling. In family counseling, information about one family member cannot be disclosed to another member without permission. Counselors protect the privacy rights of each family member. (See A.8., B.3., and B.4.d.)

B.3. Minor or Incompetent Clients

When counseling clients who are minors or individuals who are unable to give voluntary, informed consent, parents or guardians may be included in the counseling process as appropriate. Counselors act in the best interests of clients and take measures to safeguard confidentiality. (See A.3.c.)

B.4. Records

a. Requirement of Records. Counselors maintain records necessary for rendering professional services to their clients and as required by laws, regulations, or agency or institution procedures.

b. Confidentiality of Records. Counselors are responsible for securing the safety and confidentiality of any counseling records they create, maintain, transfer, or destroy whether the records are written, taped, computerized, or stored in any other medium. (See B.1.a.)

c. Permission to Record or Observe. Counselors obtain permission from clients prior to electronically recording or observing sessions. (See A.3.a.)

d. Client Access. Counselors recognize that counseling records are kept for the benefit of clients, and therefore provide access to records and copies of records when requested by competent clients, unless the records contain information that may be misleading and detrimental to the client. In situations involving multiple clients, access to records is limited to those parts of records that do not include confidential information related to another client. (See A.8., B.1.a., and B.2.b.)

e. Disclosure or Transfer. Counselors obtain written permission from clients to disclose or transfer records to legitimate third parties unless exceptions to confidentiality exist as listed in Section B.1. Steps are taken to ensure that receivers of counseling records are sensitive to their confidential nature.

B.5. Research and Training

a. Data Disguise Required. Use of data derived from counseling relationships for purposes of training, research, or publication is confined to content that is disguised to ensure the anonymity of the individuals involved. (See B.1.g. and G.3.d.)

b. Agreement for Identification. Identification of a client in a presentation or publication is permissible only when the client has reviewed the material and has agreed to its presentation or publication. (See G.3.d.)

B.6. Consultation

a. Respect for Privacy. Information obtained in a consulting relationship is discussed for professional purposes only with persons clearly concerned with the case. Written and oral reports present data germane to the purposes of the consultation, and every effort is made to protect client identity and avoid undue invasion of privacy.

b.   Cooperating Agencies. Before sharing information, counselors make efforts to ensure that there are defined policies in other agencies serving the counselor +s clients that effectively protect the confidentiality of information.

Section C: Professional Responsibility

C.1. Standards Knowledge

Counselors have a responsibility to read, understand, and follow the Code of Ethics and the Standards of Practice.

C.2. Professional Competence

a.   Boundaries of Competence. Counselors practice only within the boundaries of their competence, based on their education, training, supervised experience, state and national professional credentials, and appropriate professional experience. Counselors will demonstrate a commitment to gain knowledge, personal awareness, sensitivity, and skills pertinent to working with a diverse client population.

b.   New Specialty Areas of Practice. Counselors practice in specialty areas new to them only after appropriate education, training, and supervised experience. While developing skills in new specialty areas, counselors take steps to ensure the competence of their work and to protect others from possible harm.

c.   Qualified for Employment. Counselors accept employment only for positions for which they are qualified by education, training, supervised experience, state and national professional credentials, and appropriate professional experience. Counselors hire for professional counseling positions only individuals who are qualified and competent.

d.   Monitor Effectiveness. Counselors continually monitor their effectiveness as professionals and take steps to improve when necessary. Counselors in private practice take reasonable steps to seek out peer supervision to evaluate their efficacy as counselors.

e.   Ethical Issues Consultation. Counselors take reasonable steps to consult with other counselors or related professionals when they have questions regarding their ethical obligations or professional practice. (See H.1.)

f. Continuing Education. Counselors recognize the need for continuing education to maintain a reasonable level of awareness of current scientific and professional information in their fields of activity. They take steps to maintain competence in the skills they use, are open to new procedures, and keep current with the diverse and/or special populations with whom they work.

g. Impairment. Counselors refrain from offering or accepting professional services when their physical, mental, or emotional problems are likely to harm a client or others. They are alert to the signs of impairment, seek assistance for problems, and, if necessary, limit, suspend, or terminate their professional responsibilities. (See A.11.c.)

C.3. Advertising and Soliciting Clients

a. Accurate Advertising. There are no restrictions on advertising by counselors except those that can be specifically justified to protect the public from deceptive practices. Counselors advertise or represent their services to the public by identifying their credentials in an accurate manner that is not false, misleading, deceptive, or fraudulent. Counselors may only advertise the highest degree earned which is in counseling or a closely related field from a college or university that was accredited when the degree was awarded by one of the regional accrediting bodies recognized by the Council on Postsecondary Accreditation.

b. Testimonials. Counselors who use testimonials do not solicit them from clients or other persons who, because of their particular circumstances, may be vulnerable to undue influence.

c. Statements by Others. Counselors make reasonable efforts to ensure that statements made by others about them or the profession of counseling are accurate.

d. Recruiting Through Employment. Counselors do not use their places of employment or institutional affiliation to recruit or gain clients, supervisees, or consultees for their private practices. (See C.5.e.)

e. Products and Training Advertisements. Counselors who develop products related to their profession or conduct workshops or training events ensure that the advertisements concerning these products or events are accurate and disclose adequate information for consumers to make informed choices.

f. Promoting to Those Served. Counselors do not use counseling, teaching, training, or supervisory relationships to promote their products or training events in a manner that is deceptive or would exert undue influence on individuals who may be vulnerable. Counselors may adopt textbooks they have authored for instruction purposes.

g. Professional Association Involvement. Counselors actively participate in local, state, and national associations that foster the development and improvement of counseling.

C.4. Credentials

a. Credentials Claimed. Counselors claim or imply only professional credentials possessed and are responsible for correcting any known misrepresentations of their credentials by others. Professional credentials include graduate degrees in counseling or closely related mental health fields, accreditation of graduate programs, national voluntary certifications, government-issued certifications or licenses, ACA professional membership, or any other credential that might indicate to the public specialized knowledge or expertise in counseling.

b. ACA Professional Membership. ACA professional members may announce to the public their membership status. Regular members may not announce their ACA membership in a manner that might imply they are credentialed counselors.

c. Credential Guidelines. Counselors follow the guidelines for use of credentials that have been established by the entities that issue the credentials.

d. Misrepresentation of Credentials. Counselors do not attribute more to their credentials than the credentials represent, and do not imply that other counselors are not qualified because they do not possess certain credentials.

e. Doctoral Degrees From Other Fields. Counselors who hold a master's degree in counseling or a closely related mental health field, but hold a doctoral degree from other than counseling or a closely related field, do not use the title "Dr." in their practices and do not announce to the public in relation to their practice or status as a counselor that they hold a doctorate.

C.5. Public Responsibility

a. Nondiscrimination. Counselors do not discriminate against clients, students, or supervisees in a manner that has a negative impact based on their age, color, culture, disability, ethnic group, gender, race, religion, sexual orientation, or socioeconomic status, or for any other reason. (See A.2.a.)

b. Sexual Harassment. Counselors do not engage in sexual harassment. Sexual harassment is defined as sexual solicitation, physical advances, or verbal or nonverbal conduct that is sexual in nature, that occurs in connection with professional activities or roles, and that either (1) is unwelcome, is offensive, or creates a hostile workplace environment, and counselors know or are told this; or (2) is sufficiently severe or intense to be perceived as harassment to a reasonable person in the context. Sexual harassment can consist of a single intense or severe act or multiple persistent or pervasive acts.

c. Reports to Third Parties. Counselors are accurate, honest, and unbiased in reporting their professional activities and judgments to appropriate third parties including courts, health insurance companies, those who are the recipients of evaluation reports, and others. (See B.1.g.)

d. Media Presentations. When counselors provide advice or comment by means of public lectures, demonstrations, radio or television programs, prerecorded tapes, printed articles, mailed material, or other media, they take reasonable precautions to ensure that (1) the statements are based on appropriate professional counseling literature and practice; (2) the statements are otherwise consistent with the Code of Ethics and the Standards of Practice; and (3) the recipients of the information are not encouraged to infer that a professional counseling relationship has been established. (See C.6.b.)

e. Unjustified Gains. Counselors do not use their professional positions to seek or receive unjustified personal gains, sexual favors, unfair advantage, or unearned goods or services. (See C.3.d.)

C.6. Responsibility to Other Professionals

a. Different Approaches. Counselors are respectful of approaches to professional counseling that differ from their own. Counselors know and take into account the traditions and practices of other professional groups with which they work.

b. Personal Public Statements. When making personal statements in a public context, counselors clarify that they are speaking from their personal perspectives and that they are not speaking on behalf of all counselors or the profession. (See C.5.d.)

c. Clients Served by Others. When counselors learn that their clients are in a professional relationship with another mental health professional, they request release from clients to inform the other professionals and strive to establish positive and collaborative professional relationships. (See A.4.)

Section D: Relationships With Other Professionals

D.1. Relationships With Employers and Employees

a. Role Definition. Counselors define and describe for their employers and employees the parameters and levels of their professional roles.

b. Agreements. Counselors establish working agreements with supervisors, colleagues, and subordinates regarding counseling or clinical relationships, confidentiality, adherence to professional standards, distinction between public and private material, maintenance and dissemination of recorded information, work load, and accountability. Working agreements in each instance are specified and made known to those concerned.

c. Negative Conditions. Counselors alert their employers to conditions that may be potentially disruptive or damaging to the counselor's professional responsibilities or that may limit their effectiveness.

d. Evaluation. Counselors submit regularly to professional review and evaluation by their supervisor or the appropriate representative of the employer.

e. In-Service. Counselors are responsible for in-service development of self and staff.

f. Goals. Counselors inform their staff of goals and programs.

g. Counselors provide personnel and agency practices that respect and enhance the rights and welfare of each employee and recipient of agency services. Counselors strive to maintain the highest levels of professional services.

h. Personnel Selection and Assignment. Counselors select competent staff and assign responsibilities compatible with their skills and experiences.

i. Discrimination. Counselors, as either employers or employees, do not engage in or condone practices that are inhumane, illegal, or unjustifiable (such as considerations based on age, color, culture, disability, ethnic group, gender, race, religion, sexual orientation, or socioeconomic status) in hiring, promotion, or training. (See A.2.a. and C.5.b.)

j. Professional Conduct. Counselors have a responsibility both to clients and to the agency or institution within which services are performed to maintain high standards of professional conduct.

k. Exploitative Relationships. Counselors do not engage in exploitative relationships with individuals over whom they have supervisory, evaluative, or instructional control or authority. l. Employer Policies.

The acceptance of employment in an agency or institution implies that counselors are in agreement with its general policies and principles. Counselors strive to reach agreement with employers as to acceptable standards of conduct that allow for changes in institutional policy conducive to the growth and development of clients.

D.2. Consultation (See B.6.)

a. Consultation as an Option. Counselors may choose to consult with any other professionally competent persons about their clients. In choosing consultants, counselors avoid placing the consultant in a conflict of interest situation that would preclude the consultant being a proper party to the counselor's efforts to help the client. Should counselors be engaged in a work setting that compromises this consultation standard, they consult with other professionals whenever possible to consider justifiable alternatives.

b. Consultant Competency. Counselors are reasonably certain that they have or the organization represented has the necessary competencies and resources for giving the kind of consulting services needed and that appropriate referral resources are available.

c. Understanding With Clients. When providing consultation, counselors attempt to develop with their clients a clear understanding of problem definition, goals for change, and predicted consequences of interventions selected.

d. Consultant Goals. The consulting relationship is one in which client adaptability and growth toward self-direction are consistently encouraged and cultivated. (See A.1.b.)

D.3. Fees for Referral

a. Accepting Fees From Agency Clients. Counselors refuse a private fee or other remuneration for rendering services to persons who are entitled to such services through the counselor's employing agency or institution. The policies of a particular agency may make explicit provisions for agency clients to receive counseling services from members of its staff in private practice. In such instances, the clients must be informed of other options open to them should they seek private counseling services. (See A.10.a., A.11.b., and C.3.d.)

b. Referral Fees. Counselors do not accept a referral fee from other professionals.

D.4. Subcontractor Arrangements

When counselors work as subcontractors for counseling services for a third party, they have a duty to inform clients of the limitations of confidentiality that the organization may place on counselors in providing counseling services to clients. The limits of such confidentiality ordinarily are discussed as part of the intake session. (See B.1.e. and B.1.f.)

Section E: Evaluation, Assessment, and Interpretation

E.1. General

a. Appraisal Techniques. The primary purpose of educational and psychological assessment is to provide measures that are objective and interpretable in either comparative or absolute terms. Counselors recognize the need to interpret the statements in this section as applying to the whole range of appraisal techniques, including test and nontest data.

b. Client Welfare. Counselors promote the welfare and best interests of the client in the development, publication, and utilization of educational and psychological assessment techniques. They do not misuse assessment results and interpretations and take reasonable steps to prevent others from misusing the information these techniques provide. They respect the client's right to know the results, the interpretations made, and the bases for their conclusions and recommendations.

E.2. Competence to Use and Interpret Tests

a. Limits of Competence. Counselors recognize the limits of their competence and perform only those testing and assessment services for which they have been trained. They are familiar with reliability, validity, related standardization, error of measurement, and proper application of any technique utilized. Counselors using computer-based test interpretations are trained in the construct being measured and the specific instrument being used prior to using this type of computer application. Counselors take reasonable measures to ensure the proper use of psychological assessment techniques by persons under their supervision.

    b.   Appropriate Use. Counselors are responsible for the appropriate application, scoring, interpretation, and use of assessment instruments, whether they score and interpret such tests themselves or use computerized or other services.

    c.   Decisions Based on Results. Counselors responsible for decisions involving individuals or policies that are based on assessment results have a thorough understanding of educational and psychological measurement, including validation criteria, test research, and guidelines for test development and use.

    d.   Accurate Information. Counselors provide accurate information and avoid false claims or misconceptions when making statements about assessment instruments or techniques. Special efforts are made to avoid unwarranted connotations of such terms as IQ and grade equivalent scores. (See C.5.c.)

E.3. Informed Consent

    a.   Explanation to Clients. Prior to assessment, counselors explain the nature and purposes of assessment and the specific use of results in language the client (or other legally authorized person on behalf of the client) can understand, unless an explicit exception to this right has been agreed upon in advance. Regardless of whether scoring and interpretation are completed by counselors, by assistants, or by computer or other outside services, counselors take reasonable steps to ensure that appropriate explanations are given to the client.

    b.   Recipients of Results. The examinee's welfare, explicit understanding, and prior agreement determine the recipients of test results. Counselors include accurate and appropriate interpretations with any release of individual or group test results. (See B.1.a. and C.5.c.)

E.4. Release of Information to Competent Professionals

    a.   Misuse of Results. Counselors do not misuse assessment results, including test results, and interpretations, and take reasonable steps to prevent the misuse of such by others. (See C.5.c.)

    b.   Release of Raw Data. Counselors ordinarily release data (e.g., protocols, counseling or interview notes, or questionnaires) in which the client is identified only with the consent of the client or the client +s legal representative. Such data are usually released only to persons recognized by counselors as competent to interpret the data. (See B.1.a.)

E.5. Proper Diagnosis of Mental Disorders

a. Proper Diagnosis. Counselors take special care to provide proper diagnosis of mental disorders. Assessment techniques (including personal interview) used to determine client care (e.g., locus of treatment, type of treatment, or recommended follow-up) are carefully selected and appropriately used. (See A.3.a. and C.5.c.)

b. Cultural Sensitivity. Counselors recognize that culture affects the manner in which clients' problems are defined. Clients' socioeconomic and cultural experience is considered when diagnosing mental disorders.

E.6. Test Selection

a. Appropriateness of Instruments. Counselors carefully consider the validity, reliability, psychometric limitations, and appropriateness of instruments when selecting tests for use in a given situation or with a particular client.

b. Culturally Diverse Populations. Counselors are cautious when selecting tests for culturally diverse populations to avoid inappropriateness of testing that may be outside of socialized behavioral or cognitive patterns.

E.7. Conditions of Test Administration

a. Administration Conditions. Counselors administer tests under the same conditions that were established in their standardization. When tests are not administered under standard conditions or when unusual behavior or irregularities occur during the testing session, those conditions are noted in interpretation, and the results may be designated as invalid or of questionable validity.

b. Computer Administration. Counselors are responsible for ensuring that administration programs function properly to provide clients with accurate results when a computer or other electronic methods are used for test administration. (See A.12.b.)

c. Unsupervised Test Taking. Counselors do not permit unsupervised or inadequately supervised use of tests or assessments unless the tests or assessments are designed, intended, and validated for self-administration and/or scoring.

d.   Disclosure of Favorable Conditions. Prior to test administration, conditions that produce most favorable test results are made known to the examinee.

E.8. Diversity in Testing

Counselors are cautious in using assessment techniques, making evaluations, and interpreting the performance of populations not represented in the norm group on which an instrument was standardized. They recognize the effects of age, color, culture, disability, ethnic group, gender, race, religion, sexual orientation, and socioeconomic status on test administration and interpretation and place test results in proper perspective with other relevant factors. (See A.2.a.)

E.9. Test Scoring and Interpretation

a.   Reporting Reservations. In reporting assessment results, counselors indicate any reservations that exist regarding validity or reliability because of the circumstances of the assessment or the inappropriateness of the norms for the person tested.

b.   Research Instruments. Counselors exercise caution when interpreting the results of research instruments possessing insufficient technical data to support respondent results. The specific purposes for the use of such instruments are stated explicitly to the examinee.

c.   Testing Services. Counselors who provide test scoring and test interpretation services to support the assessment process confirm the validity of such interpretations. They accurately describe the purpose, norms, validity, reliability, and applications of the procedures and any special qualifications applicable to their use. The public offering of an automated test interpretations service is considered a professional-to-professional consultation. The formal responsibility of the consultant is to the consultee, but the ultimate and overriding responsibility is to the client.

E.10.   Test Security

Counselors maintain the integrity and security of tests and other assessment techniques consistent with legal and contractual obligations. Counselors do not appropriate, reproduce, or modify published tests or parts thereof without acknowledgment and permission from the publisher.

E.11.   Obsolete Tests and Outdated Test Results

Counselors do not use data or test results that are obsolete or outdated for the current purpose. Counselors make every effort to prevent the misuse of obsolete measures and test data by others.

E.12.   Test Construction

Counselors use established scientific procedures, relevant standards, and current professional knowledge for test design in the development, publication, and utilization of educational and psychological assessment techniques.

Section F: Teaching, Training, and Supervision

F.1. Counselor Educators and Trainers

    a.   Educators as Teachers and Practitioners. Counselors who are responsible for developing, implementing, and supervising educational programs are skilled as teachers and practitioners. They are knowledgeable regarding the ethical, legal, and regulatory aspects of the profession, are skilled in applying that knowledge, and make students and supervisees aware of their responsibilities. Counselors conduct counselor education and training programs in an ethical manner and serve as role models for professional behavior. Counselor educators should make an effort to infuse material related to human diversity into all courses and/or workshops that are designed to promote the development of professional counselors.

    b.   Relationship Boundaries With Students and Supervisees. Counselors clearly define and maintain ethical, professional, and social relationship boundaries with their students and supervisees. They are aware of the differential in power that exists and the student's or supervisee's possible incomprehension of that power differential. Counselors explain to students and supervisees the potential for the relationship to become exploitive.

c. Sexual Relationships. Counselors do not engage in sexual relationships with students or supervisees and do not subject them to sexual harassment. (See A.6. and C.5.b)

d. Contributions to Research. Counselors give credit to students or supervisees for their contributions to research and scholarly projects. Credit is given through coauthorship, acknowledgment, footnote statement, or other appropriate means, in accordance with such contributions. (See G.4.b. and G.4.c.)

e. Close Relatives. Counselors do not accept close relatives as students or supervisees.

f. Supervision Preparation. Counselors who offer clinical supervision services are adequately prepared in supervision methods and techniques. Counselors who are doctoral students serving as practicum or internship supervisors to master's level students are adequately prepared and supervised by the training program.

g. Responsibility for Services to Clients. Counselors who supervise the counseling services of others take reasonable measures to ensure that counseling services provided to clients are professional.

h. Endorsement. Counselors do not endorse students or supervisees for certification, licensure, employment, or completion of an academic or training program if they believe students or supervisees are not qualified for the endorsement. Counselors take reasonable steps to assist students or supervisees who are not qualified for endorsement to become qualified.

F.2. Counselor Education and Training Programs

a. Orientation. Prior to admission, counselors orient prospective students to the counselor education or training program +s expectations, including but not limited to the following: (1) the type and level of skill acquisition required for successful completion of the training, (2) subject matter to be covered, (3) basis for evaluation, (4) training components that encourage self-growth or self-disclosure as part of the training process, (5) the type of supervision settings and requirements of the sites for required clinical field experiences, (6) student and supervisee evaluation and dismissal policies and procedures, and (7) up-to-date employment prospects for graduates.

b. Integration of Study and Practice. Counselors establish counselor education and training programs that integrate academic study and supervised practice.

c.   Evaluation. Counselors clearly state to students and supervisees, in advance of training, the levels of competency expected, appraisal methods, and timing of evaluations for both didactic and experiential components. Counselors provide students and supervisees with periodic performance appraisal and evaluation feedback throughout the training program.

d.   Teaching Ethics. Counselors make students and supervisees aware of the ethical responsibilities and standards of the profession and the students + and supervisees' ethical responsibilities to the profession. (See C.1. and F.3.e.)

e.   Peer Relationships. When students or supervisees are assigned to lead counseling groups or provide clinical supervision for their peers, counselors take steps to ensure that students and supervisees placed in these roles do not have personal or adverse relationships with peers and that they understand they have the same ethical obligations as counselor educators, trainers, and supervisors. Counselors make every effort to ensure that the rights of peers are not compromised when students or supervisees are assigned to lead counseling groups or provide clinical supervision.

f.   Varied Theoretical Positions. Counselors present varied theoretical positions so that students and supervisees may make comparisons and have opportunities to develop their own positions. Counselors provide information concerning the scientific bases of professional practice. (See C.6.a.)

g.   Field Placements. Counselors develop clear policies within their training program regarding field placement and other clinical experiences. Counselors provide clearly stated roles and responsibilities for the student or supervisee, the site supervisor, and the program supervisor. They confirm that site supervisors are qualified to provide supervision and are informed of their professional and ethical responsibilities in this role.

h.   Dual Relationships as Supervisors. Counselors avoid dual relationships such as performing the role of site supervisor and training program supervisor in the student's or supervisee's training program. Counselors do not accept any form of professional services, fees, commissions, reimbursement, or remuneration from a site for student or supervisee placement.

i.   Diversity in Programs. Counselors are responsive to their institution's and program's recruitment and retention needs for training program administrators, faculty, and students with diverse backgrounds and special needs. (See A.2.a.)

F.3. Students and Supervisees

a. Limitations. Counselors, through ongoing evaluation and appraisal, are aware of the academic and personal limitations of students and supervisees that might impede performance. Counselors assist students and supervisees in securing remedial assistance when needed, and dismiss from the training program supervisees who are unable to provide competent service due to academic or personal limitations. Counselors seek professional consultation and document their decision to dismiss or refer students or supervisees for assistance. Counselors ensure that students and supervisees have recourse to address decisions made to require them to seek assistance or to dismiss them.

b. Self-Growth Experiences. Counselors use professional judgment when designing training experiences conducted by the counselors themselves that require student and supervisee self-growth or self-disclosure. Safeguards are provided so that students and supervisees are aware of the ramifications their self-disclosure may have on counselors whose primary role as teacher, trainer, or supervisor requires acting on ethical obligations to the profession. Evaluative components of experiential training experiences explicitly delineate predetermined academic standards that are separate and do not depend on the student's level of self-disclosure. (See A.6.)

c. Counseling for Students and Supervisees. If students or supervisees request counseling, supervisors or counselor educators provide them with acceptable referrals. Supervisors or counselor educators do not serve as counselor to students or supervisees over whom they hold administrative, teaching, or evaluative roles unless this is a brief role associated with a training experience. (See A.6.b.)

d. Clients of Students and Supervisees. Counselors make every effort to ensure that the clients at field placements are aware of the services rendered and the qualifications of the students and supervisees rendering those services. Clients receive professional disclosure information and are informed of the limits of confidentiality. Client permission is obtained in order for the students and supervisees to use any information concerning the counseling relationship in the training process. (See B.1.e.)

e. Standards for Students and Supervisees. Students and supervisees preparing to become counselors adhere to the Code of Ethics and the Standards of Practice. Students and supervisees have the same obligations to clients as those required of counselors. (See H.1.)

Section G: Research and Publication

G.1. Research Responsibilities

 a. Use of Human Subjects. Counselors plan, design, conduct, and report research in a manner consistent with pertinent ethical principles, federal and state laws, host institutional regulations, and scientific standards governing research with human subjects. Counselors design and conduct research that reflects cultural sensitivity appropriateness.

 b. Deviation From Standard Practices. Counselors seek consultation and observe stringent safeguards to protect the rights of research participants when a research problem suggests a deviation from standard acceptable practices. (See B.6.)

 c. Precautions to Avoid Injury. Counselors who conduct research with human subjects are responsible for the subjects' welfare throughout the experiment and take reasonable precautions to avoid causing injurious psychological, physical, or social effects to their subjects.

 d. Principal Researcher Responsibility. The ultimate responsibility for ethical research practice lies with the principal researcher. All others involved in the research activities share ethical obligations and full responsibility for their own actions.

 e. Minimal Interference. Counselors take reasonable precautions to avoid causing disruptions in subjects' lives due to participation in research.

 f. Diversity. Counselors are sensitive to diversity and research issues with special populations. They seek consultation when appropriate. (See A.2.a. and B.6.)

G.2. Informed Consent

 a. Topics Disclosed. In obtaining informed consent for research, counselors use language that is understandable to research participants and that (1) accurately explains the purpose and procedures to be followed; (2) identifies any procedures that are experimental or relatively untried; (3) describes the attendant discomforts and risks; (4) describes the benefits or changes in individuals or organizations that might be reasonably expected; (5) discloses appropriate alternative procedures that would be advantageous for subjects; (6) offers to answer any inquiries concerning the procedures; (7) describes any limitations on confidentiality; and (8) instructs that subjects are free to withdraw their consent and to discontinue participation in the project at any time. (See B.1.f.)

b. Deception. Counselors do not conduct research involving deception unless alternative procedures are not feasible and the prospective value of the research justifies the deception. When the methodological requirements of a study necessitate concealment or deception, the investigator is required to explain clearly the reasons for this action as soon as possible.

c. Voluntary Participation. Participation in research is typically voluntary and without any penalty for refusal to participate. Involuntary participation is appropriate only when it can be demonstrated that participation will have no harmful effects on subjects and is essential to the investigation.

d. Confidentiality of Information. Information obtained about research participants during the course of an investigation is confidential. When the possibility exists that others may obtain access to such information, ethical research practice requires that the possibility, together with the plans for protecting confidentiality, be explained to participants as a part of the procedure for obtaining informed consent. (See B.1.e.)

e. Persons Incapable of Giving Informed Consent. When a person is incapable of giving informed consent, counselors provide an appropriate explanation, obtain agreement for participation, and obtain appropriate consent from a legally authorized person.

f. Commitments to Participants. Counselors take reasonable measures to honor all commitments to research participants.

g. Explanations After Data Collection. After data are collected, counselors provide participants with full clarification of the nature of the study to remove any misconceptions. Where scientific or human values justify delaying or withholding information, counselors take reasonable measures to avoid causing harm.

h. Agreements to Cooperate. Counselors who agree to cooperate with another individual in research or publication incur an obligation to cooperate as promised in terms of punctuality of performance and with regard to the completeness and accuracy of the information required.

i. Informed Consent for Sponsors. In the pursuit of research, counselors give sponsors, institutions, and publication channels the same respect and opportunity for giving informed consent that they accord to individual research participants. Counselors are aware of their obligation to future research workers and ensure that host institutions are given feedback information and proper acknowledgment.

G.3. Reporting Results

a. Information Affecting Outcome. When reporting research results, counselors explicitly mention all variables and conditions known to the investigator that may have affected the outcome of a study or the interpretation of data.

b. Accurate Results. Counselors plan, conduct, and report research accurately and in a manner that minimizes the possibility that results will be misleading. They provide thorough discussions of the limitations of their data and alternative hypotheses. Counselors do not engage in fraudulent research, distort data, misrepresent data, or deliberately bias their results.

c. Obligation to Report Unfavorable Results. Counselors communicate to other counselors the results of any research judged to be of professional value. Results that reflect unfavorably on institutions, programs, services, prevailing opinions, or vested interests are not withheld.

d. Identity of Subjects. Counselors who supply data, aid in the research of another person, report research results, or make original data available take due care to disguise the identity of respective subjects in the absence of specific authorization from the subjects to do otherwise. (See B.1.g. and B.5.a.)

e. Replication Studies. Counselors are obligated to make available sufficient original research data to qualified professionals who may wish to replicate the study.

G.4. Publication

a. Recognition of Others. When conducting and reporting research, counselors are familiar with and give recognition to previous work on the topic, observe copyright laws, and give full credit to those to whom credit is due. (See F.1.d. and G.4.c.)

b. Contributors. Counselors give credit through joint authorship, acknowledgment, footnote statements, or other appropriate means to those who have contributed significantly to research or concept development in accordance with such contributions. The principal contributor is listed first and minor technical or professional contributions are acknowledged in notes or introductory statements.

c. Student Research. For an article that is substantially based on a student +s dissertation or thesis, the student is listed as the principal author. (See F.1.d. and G.4.a.)

    d.   Duplicate Submission. Counselors submit manuscripts for consideration to only one journal at a time. Manuscripts that are published in whole or in substantial part in another journal or published work are not submitted for publication without acknowledgment and permission from the previous publication.

    e.   Professional Review. Counselors who review material submitted for publication, research, or other scholarly purposes respect the confidentiality and proprietary rights of those who submitted it.

Section H: Resolving Ethical Issues

H.1. Knowledge of Standards

Counselors are familiar with the Code of Ethics and the Standards of Practice and other applicable ethics codes from other professional organizations of which they are member, or from certification and licensure bodies. Lack of knowledge or misunderstanding of an ethical responsibility is not a defense against a charge of unethical conduct. (See F.3.e.)

H.2. Suspected Violations

    a.   Ethical Behavior Expected. Counselors expect professional associates to adhere to the Code of Ethics. When counselors possess reasonable cause that raises doubts as to whether a counselor is acting in an ethical manner, they take appropriate action. (See H.2.d. and H.2.e.)

    b.   Consultation. When uncertain as to whether a particular situation or course of action may be in violation of the Code of Ethics, counselors consult with other counselors who are knowledgeable about ethics, with colleagues, or with appropriate authorities.

    c.   Organization Conflicts. If the demands of an organization with which counselors are affiliated pose a conflict with the Code of Ethics, counselors specify the nature of such conflicts and express to their supervisors or other responsible officials their commitment to the Code of Ethics. When possible, counselors work toward change within the organization to allow full adherence to the Code of Ethics.

    d.   Informal Resolution. When counselors have reasonable cause to believe that another counselor is violating an ethical standard, they attempt to first resolve the issue informally with the other counselor if feasible, providing that such action does not violate confidentiality rights that may be involved.

e. Reporting Suspected Violations. When an informal resolution is not appropriate or feasible, counselors, upon reasonable cause, take action such as reporting the suspected ethical violation to state or national ethics committees, unless this action conflicts with confidentiality rights that cannot be resolved.

f. Unwarranted Complaints. Counselors do not initiate, participate in, or encourage the filing of ethics complaints that are unwarranted or intend to harm a counselor rather than to protect clients or the public.

H.3. Cooperation With Ethics Committees

Counselors assist in the process of enforcing the Code of Ethics. Counselors cooperate with investigations, proceedings, and requirements of the ACA Ethics Committee or ethics committees of other duly constituted associations or boards having jurisdiction over those charged with a violation. Counselors are familiar with the ACA Policies and Procedures and use it as a reference in assisting the enforcement of the Code of Ethics.

ACA Standards of Practice

All members of the American Counseling Association (ACA) are required to adhere to the Standards of Practice and the Code of Ethics. The Standards of Practice represent minimal behavioral statements of the Code of Ethics. Members should refer to the applicable section of the Code of Ethics for further interpretation and amplification of the applicable Standard of Practice.

Section A: The Counseling Relationship
Section B: Confidentiality
Section C: Professional Responsibility
Section D: Relationship With Other Professionals
Section E: Evaluation, Assessment and Interpretation
Section F: Teaching, Training, and Supervision
Section G: Research and Publication
Section H: Resolving Ethical Issues

Section A: The Counseling Relationship

Standard of Practice One (SP-1):

Nondiscrimination. Counselors respect diversity and must not discriminate against clients because of age, color, culture, disability, ethnic group, gender, race, religion, sexual orientation, marital status, or socioeconomic status. (See A.2.a.)

Standard of Practice Two (SP-2):

Disclosure to Clients. Counselors must adequately inform clients, preferably in writing, regarding the counseling process and counseling relationship at or before the time it begins and throughout the relationship. (See A.3.a.)

Standard of Practice Three (SP-3):

Dual Relationships. Counselors must make every effort to avoid dual relationships with clients that could impair their professional judgment or increase the risk of harm to clients. When a dual relationship cannot be avoided, counselors must take appropriate steps to ensure that judgment is not impaired and that no exploitation occurs. (See A.6.a. and A.6.b.)

Standard of Practice Four (SP-4):

Sexual Intimacies With Clients. Counselors must not engage in any type of sexual intimacies with current clients and must not engage in sexual intimacies with former clients within a minimum of 2 years after terminating the counseling relationship. Counselors who engage in such relationship after 2 years following termination have the responsibility to examine and document thoroughly that such relations did not have an exploitative nature.

Standard of Practice Five (SP-5):

Protecting Clients During Group Work. Counselors must take steps to protect clients from physical or psychological trauma resulting from interactions during group work. (See A.9 b.)

Standard of Practice Six (SP-6):

Advance Understanding of Fees. Counselors must explain to clients, prior to their entering the counseling relationship, financial arrangements related to professional services. (See A.10. a.-d. and A.11.c.)

Standard of Practice Seven (SP-7):

Termination. Counselors must assist in making appropriate arrangements for the continuation of treatment of clients, when necessary, following termination of counseling relationships. (See A.11.a.)

Standard of Practice Eight (SP-8):

Inability to Assist Clients. Counselors must avoid entering or immediately terminate a counseling relationship if it is determined that they are unable to be of professional assistance to a client. The counselor may assist in making an appropriate referral for the client. (See A.11.b.)

Section B: Confidentiality

Standard of Practice Nine (SP-9):

Confidentiality Requirement. Counselors must keep information related to counseling services confidential unless disclosure is in the best interest of clients, is required for the welfare of others, or is required by law. When disclosure is required, only information that is essential is revealed and the client is informed of such disclosure. (See B.1. a.+f.)

Standard of Practice Ten (SP-10):

Confidentiality Requirements for Subordinates. Counselors must take measures to ensure that privacy and confidentiality of clients are maintained by subordinates. (See B.1.h.)

Standard of Practice Eleven (SP-11):

Confidentiality in Group Work. Counselors must clearly communicate to group members that confidentiality cannot be guaranteed in group work. (See B.2.a.)

Standard of Practice Twelve (SP-12):

Confidentiality in Family Counseling. Counselors must not disclose information about one family member in counseling to another family member without prior consent. (See B.2.b.)

Standard of Practice Thirteen (SP-13):

Confidentiality of Records. Counselors must maintain appropriate confidentiality in creating, storing, accessing, transferring, and disposing of counseling records. (See B.4.b.)

Standard of Practice Fourteen (SP-14):

Permission to Record or Observe. Counselors must obtain prior consent from clients in order to record electronically or observe sessions. (See B.4.c.)

Standard of Practice Fifteen (SP-15):

Disclosure or Transfer of Records. Counselors must obtain client consent to disclose or transfer records to third parties, unless exceptions listed in SP-9 exist. (See B.4.e.)

Standard of Practice Sixteen (SP-16):

Data Disguise Required. Counselors must disguise the identity of the client when using data for training, research, or publication. (See B.5.a.)

Section C: Professional Responsibility

Standard of Practice Seventeen (SP-17):

Boundaries of Competence. Counselors must practice only within the boundaries of their competence. (See C.2.a.)

Standard of Practice Eighteen (SP-18):

Continuing Education. Counselors must engage in continuing education to maintain their professional competence. (See C.2.f.)

Standard of Practice Nineteen (SP-19):

Impairment of Professionals. Counselors must refrain from offering professional services when their personal problems or conflicts may cause harm to a client or others. (See C.2.g.)

Standard of Practice Twenty (SP-20):

Accurate Advertising. Counselors must accurately represent their credentials and services when advertising. (See C.3.a.)

Standard of Practice Twenty-One (SP-21):

Recruiting Through Employment. Counselors must not use their place of employment or institutional affiliation to recruit clients for their private practices. (See C.3.d.)

Standard of Practice Twenty-Two (SP-22):

Credentials Claimed. Counselors must claim or imply only professional credentials possessed and must correct any known misrepresentations of their credentials by others. (See C.4.a.)

Standard of Practice Twenty-Three (SP-23):

Sexual Harassment. Counselors must not engage in sexual harassment. (See C.5.b.)

Standard of Practice Twenty-Four (SP-24):

Unjustified Gains. Counselors must not use their professional positions to seek or receive unjustified personal gains, sexual favors, unfair advantage, or unearned goods or services. (See C.5.e.)

Standard of Practice Twenty-Five (SP-25):

Clients Served by Others. With the consent of the client, counselors must inform other mental health professionals serving the same client that a counseling relationship between the counselor and client exists. (See C.6.c.)

Standard of Practice Twenty-Six (SP-26):

Negative Employment Conditions. Counselors must alert their employers to institutional policy or conditions that may be potentially disruptive or damaging to the counselor +s professional responsibilities, or that may limit their effectiveness or deny clients' rights. (See D.1.c.)

Standard of Practice Twenty-Seven (SP-27):

Personnel Selection and Assignment. Counselors must select competent staff and must assign responsibilities compatible with staff skills and experiences. (See D.1.h.)

Standard of Practice Twenty-Eight (SP-28):

Exploitative Relationships With Subordinates. Counselors must not engage in exploitative relationships with individuals over whom they have supervisory, evaluative, or instructional control or authority. (See D.1.k.)

Section D: Relationship With Other Professionals

Standard of Practice Twenty-Nine (SP-29):

Accepting Fees From Agency Clients. Counselors must not accept fees or other remuneration for consultation with persons entitled to such services through the counselor +s employing agency or institution. (See D.3.a.)

Standard of Practice Thirty (SP-30):

Referral Fees. Counselors must not accept referral fees. (See D.3.b.)

Section E: Evaluation, Assessment and Interpretation

Standard of Practice Thirty-One (SP-31):

Limits of Competence. Counselors must perform only testing and assessment services for which they are competent. Counselors must not allow the use of psychological assessment techniques by unqualified persons under their supervision. (See E.2.a.)

Standard of Practice Thirty-Two (SP-32)

Appropriate Use of Assessment Instruments. Counselors must use assessment instruments in the manner for which they were intended. (See E.2.b.)

Standard of Practice Thirty-Three (SP-33):

Assessment Explanations to Clients. Counselors must provide explanations to clients prior to assessment about the nature and purposes of assessment and the specific uses of results. (See E.3.a.)

Standard of Practice Thirty-Four (SP-34):

Recipients of Test Results. Counselors must ensure that accurate and appropriate interpretations accompany any release of testing and assessment information. (See E.3.b.)

Standard of Practice Thirty-Five (SP-35):

Obsolete Tests and Outdated Test Results. Counselors must not base their assessment or intervention decisions or recommendations on data or test results that are obsolete or outdated for the current purpose. (See E.11.)

Section F: Teaching, Training, and Supervision

Standard of Practice Thirty-Six (SP-36):

Sexual Relationships With Students or Supervisees. Counselors must not engage in sexual relationships with their students and supervisees. (See F.1.c.)

Standard of Practice Thirty-Seven (SP-37):

Credit for Contributions to Research. Counselors must give credit to students or supervisees for their contributions to research and scholarly projects. (See F.1.d.)

Standard of Practice Thirty-Eight (SP-38):

Supervision Preparation. Counselors who offer clinical supervision services must be trained and prepared in supervision methods and techniques. (See F.1.f.)

Standard of Practice Thirty-Nine (SP-39):

Evaluation Information. Counselors must clearly state to students and supervisees in advance of training the levels of competency expected, appraisal methods, and timing of evaluations. Counselors must provide students and supervisees with periodic performance appraisal and evaluation feedback throughout the training program. (See F.2.c.)

Standard of Practice Forty (SP-40):

Peer Relationships in Training. Counselors must make every effort to ensure that the rights of peers are not violated when students and supervisees are assigned to lead counseling groups or provide clinical supervision. (See F.2.e.)

Standard of Practice Forty-One (SP-41):

Limitations of Students and Supervisees. Counselors must assist students and supervisees in securing remedial assistance, when needed, and must dismiss from the training program students and supervisees who are unable to provide competent service due to academic or personal limitations. (See F.3.a.)

Standard of Practice Forty-Two (SP-42):

Self-Growth Experiences. Counselors who conduct experiences for students or supervisees that include self-growth or self-disclosure must inform participants of counselors + ethical obligations to the profession and must not grade participants based on their nonacademic performance. (See F.3.b.)

Standard of Practice Forty-Three (SP-43):

Standards for Students and Supervisees. Students and supervisees preparing to become counselors must adhere to the Code of Ethics and the Standards of Practice of counselors. (See F.3.e.)

Section G: Research and Publication

Standard of Practice Forty-Four (SP-44):

Precautions to Avoid Injury in Research. Counselors must avoid causing physical, social, or psychological harm or injury to subjects in research. (See G.1.c.)

Standard of Practice Forty-Five (SP-45):

Confidentiality of Research Information. Counselors must keep confidential information obtained about research participants. (See G.2.d.)

Standard of Practice Forty-Six (SP-46):

Information Affecting Research Outcome. Counselors must report all variables and conditions known to the investigator that may have affected research data or outcomes. (See G.3.a.)

Standard of Practice Forty-Seven (SP-47):

Accurate Research Results. Counselors must not distort or misrepresent research data, nor fabricate or intentionally bias research results. (See G.3.b.)

Standard of Practice Forty-Eight (SP-48):

Publication Contributors. Counselors must give appropriate credit to those who have contributed to research. (See G.4.a. and G.4.b.)

Section H: Resolving Ethical Issues

Standard of Practice Forty-Nine (SP-49):

Ethical Behavior Expected. Counselors must take appropriate action when they possess reasonable cause that raises doubts as to whether counselors or other mental health professionals are acting in an ethical manner. (See H.2.a.)

Standard of Practice Fifty (SP-50):

Unwarranted Complaints. Counselors must not initiate, participate in, or encourage the filing of ethics complaints that are unwarranted or intended to harm a mental health professional rather than to protect clients or the public. (See H.2.f.)

Standard of Practice Fifty-One (SP-51):

Cooperation With Ethics Committees. Counselors must cooperate with investigations, proceedings, and requirements of the ACA Ethics Committee or ethics committees of other duly constituted associations or boards having jurisdiction over those charged with a violation. (See H.3.)

References

The following documents are available to counselors as resources to guide them in their practices. These resources are not a part of the Code of Ethics and the Standards of Practice.

American Association for Counseling and Development/Association for Measurement and Evaluation in Counseling and Development. (1989). The responsibilities of users of standardized tests (rev.). Washington, DC: Author.

American Counseling Association. (1995) (Note: This is ACA's previous edition of its ethics code). Ethical standards. Alexandria, VA: Author.

American Psychological Association. (1985). Standards for educational and psychological testing (rev.). Washington, DC: Author.

Joint Committee on Testing Practices. (1988). Code of fair testing practices in education. Washington, DC: Author.

National Board for Certified Counselors. (1989). National Board for Certified Counselors code of ethics. Alexandria, VA: Author.

Prediger, D. J. (Ed.). (1993, March). Multicultural assessment standards. Alexandria, VA: Association for Assessment in Counseling.

Appendix A-2
Ethical Principles of Psychologists and Code of Conduct

History and Effective Date

Effective date June 1, 2003.

TABLE OF CONTENTS

INTRODUCTION AND APPLICABILITY

PREAMBLE

GENERAL PRINCIPLES

Principle A: Beneficence and Nonmaleficence
Principle B: Fidelity and Responsibility
Principle C: Integrity
Principle D: Justice
Principle E: Respect for People's Rights and Dignity

ETHICAL STANDARDS

INTRODUCTION AND APPLICABILITY

The American Psychological Association's (APA's) Ethical Principles of Psychologists and Code of Conduct (hereinafter referred to as the Ethics Code) consists of an Introduction, a Preamble, five General Principles (A - E), and specific Ethical Standards. The Introduction discusses the intent, organization, procedural considerations, and scope of application of the Ethics Code. The Preamble and General Principles are aspirational goals to guide psychologists toward the highest ideals of psychology. Although the Preamble and General Principles are not themselves enforceable rules, they should be considered by psychologists in arriving at an ethical course of action. The Ethical Standards set forth enforceable rules for conduct as psychologists. Most of the Ethical Standards are written broadly, in order to apply to psychologists in varied roles, although the application of an Ethical Standard may vary depending on the context. The Ethical Standards are not exhaustive. The fact that a given conduct is not specifically addressed by an Ethical Standard does not mean that it is necessarily either ethical or unethical.

This Ethics Code applies only to psychologists' activities that are part of their scientific, educational, or professional roles as psychologists. Areas covered include but are not limited to the clinical, counseling, and school practice of psychology; research; teaching; supervision of trainees; public service; policy development; social intervention; development of assessment instruments; conducting assessments; educational counseling; organizational consulting; forensic activities; program design and evaluation; and administration. This Ethics Code applies to these activities across a variety of contexts, such as in person, postal, telephone, internet, and other electronic transmissions. These activities shall be distinguished from the purely private conduct of psychologists, which is not within the purview of the Ethics Code.

Membership in the APA commits members and student affiliates to comply with the standards of the APA Ethics Code and to the rules and procedures used to enforce them. Lack of awareness or misunderstanding of an Ethical Standard is not itself a defense to a charge of unethical conduct.

The procedures for filing, investigating, and resolving complaints of unethical conduct are described in the current Rules and Procedures of the APA Ethics Committee. APA may impose sanctions on its members for violations of the standards of the Ethics Code, including termination of APA membership, and may notify other bodies and individuals of its actions. Actions that violate the standards of the Ethics Code may also lead to the imposition of sanctions on psychologists or students whether or not they are APA members by bodies other than APA, including state psychological associations, other professional groups, psychology boards, other state or federal agencies, and payors for health services. In addition, APA may take action against a member after his or her conviction of a felony, expulsion or suspension from an affiliated state psychological association, or suspension or loss of licensure. When the sanction to be imposed by APA is less than expulsion, the 2001 Rules and Procedures do not guarantee an opportunity for an in-person hearing, but generally provide that complaints will be resolved only on the basis of a submitted record.

The Ethics Code is intended to provide guidance for psychologists and standards of professional conduct that can be applied by the APA and by other bodies that choose to adopt them. The Ethics Code is not intended to be a basis of civil liability. Whether a psychologist has violated the Ethics Code standards does not by itself determine whether the psychologist is legally liable in a court action, whether a contract is enforceable, or whether other legal consequences occur.

The modifiers used in some of the standards of this Ethics Code (e.g., reasonably, appropriate, potentially) are included in the standards when they would (1) allow professional judgment on the part of psychologists, (2) eliminate injustice or inequality that would occur without the modifier, (3) ensure applicability across the broad range of activities conducted by psychologists, or (4) guard against a set of rigid rules that might be quickly outdated. As used in this Ethics Code, the term reasonable means the prevailing professional judgment of psychologists engaged in similar activities in similar circumstances, given the knowledge the psychologist had or should have had at the time.

In the process of making decisions regarding their professional behavior, psychologists must consider this Ethics Code in addition to applicable laws and psychology board regulations. In applying the Ethics Code to their professional work, psychologists may consider other materials and guidelines that have been adopted or endorsed by scientific and professional psychological organizations and the dictates of their own conscience, as well as consult with others within the field. If this Ethics Code establishes a higher standard of conduct than is required by law, psychologists must meet the higher ethical standard. If psychologists' ethical responsibilities conflict with law, regulations, or other governing legal authority, psychologists make known their commitment to this Ethics Code and take steps to resolve the conflict in a responsible manner. If the conflict is unresolvable via such means, psychologists may adhere to the requirements of the law, regulations, or other governing authority in keeping with basic principles of human rights.

PREAMBLE

Psychologists are committed to increasing scientific and professional knowledge of behavior and people's understanding of themselves and others and to the use of such knowledge to improve the condition of individuals, organizations, and society. Psychologists respect and protect civil and human rights and the central importance of freedom of inquiry and expression in research, teaching, and publication. They strive to help the public in developing informed judgments and choices concerning human behavior. In doing so, they perform many roles, such as researcher, educator, diagnostician, therapist, supervisor, consultant, administrator, social interventionist, and expert witness. This Ethics Code provides a common set of principles and standards upon which psychologists build their professional and scientific work.

This Ethics Code is intended to provide specific standards to cover most situations encountered by psychologists. It has as its goals the welfare and protection of the individuals and groups with whom psychologists work and the education of members, students, and the public regarding ethical standards of the discipline.

The development of a dynamic set of ethical standards for psychologists' work-related conduct requires a personal commitment and lifelong effort to act ethically; to encourage ethical behavior by students, supervisees, employees, and colleagues; and to consult with others concerning ethical problems.

GENERAL PRINCIPLES

This section consists of General Principles. General Principles, as opposed to Ethical Standards, are aspirational in nature. Their intent is to guide and inspire psychologists toward the very highest ethical ideals of the profession. General Principles, in contrast to Ethical Standards, do not represent obligations and should not form the basis for imposing sanctions. Relying upon General Principles for either of these reasons distorts both their meaning and purpose.

Principle A: Beneficence and Nonmaleficence

Psychologists strive to benefit those with whom they work and take care to do no harm. In their professional actions, psychologists seek to safeguard the welfare and rights of those with whom they interact professionally and other affected persons, and the welfare of animal subjects of research. When conflicts occur among psychologists' obligations or concerns, they attempt to resolve these conflicts in a responsible fashion that avoids or minimizes harm. Because psychologists' scientific and professional judgments and actions may affect the lives of others, they are alert to and guard against personal, financial, social, organizational, or political factors that might lead to misuse of their influence. Psychologists strive to be aware of the possible effect of their own physical and mental health on their ability to help those with whom they work.

Principle B: Fidelity and Responsibility

Psychologists establish relationships of trust with those with whom they work. They are aware of their professional and scientific responsibilities to society and to the specific communities in which they work. Psychologists uphold professional standards of conduct, clarify their professional roles and obligations, accept appropriate responsibility for their behavior, and seek to manage conflicts of interest that could lead to exploitation or harm. Psychologists consult with, refer to, or cooperate with other professionals and institutions to the extent needed to serve the best interests of those with whom they work. They are concerned about the ethical compliance of their colleagues' scientific and professional conduct. Psychologists strive to contribute a portion of their professional time for little or no compensation or personal advantage.

Principle C: Integrity

Psychologists seek to promote accuracy, honesty, and truthfulness in the science, teaching, and practice of psychology. In these activities psychologists do not steal, cheat, or engage in fraud, subterfuge, or intentional misrepresentation of fact. Psychologists strive to keep their promises and to avoid unwise or unclear commitments. In situations in which deception may be ethically justifiable to maximize benefits and minimize harm, psychologists have a serious obligation to consider the need for, the possible consequences of, and their responsibility to correct any resulting mistrust or other harmful effects that arise from the use of such techniques.

Principle D: Justice

Psychologists recognize that fairness and justice entitle all persons to access to and benefit from the contributions of psychology and to equal quality in the processes, procedures, and services being conducted by psychologists. Psychologists exercise reasonable judgment and take precautions to ensure that their potential biases, the boundaries of their competence, and the limitations of their expertise do not lead to or condone unjust practices.

Principle E: Respect for People's Rights and Dignity

Psychologists respect the dignity and worth of all people, and the rights of individuals to privacy, confidentiality, and self-determination. Psychologists are aware that special safeguards may be necessary to protect the rights and welfare of persons or communities whose vulnerabilities impair autonomous decision making. Psychologists are aware of and respect cultural, individual, and role differences, including those based on age, gender, gender identity, race, ethnicity, culture, national origin, religion, sexual orientation, disability, language, and socioeconomic status and consider these factors when working with members of such groups. Psychologists try to eliminate the effect on their work of biases based on those factors, and they do not knowingly participate in or condone activities of others based upon such prejudices.

ETHICAL STANDARDS

1. Resolving Ethical Issues
1.01 Misuse of Psychologists' Work
>If psychologists learn of misuse or misrepresentation of their work, they take reasonable steps to correct or minimize the misuse or misrepresentation.

1.02 Conflicts Between Ethics and Law, Regulations, or Other Governing Legal Authority
>If psychologists' ethical responsibilities conflict with law, regulations, or other governing legal authority, psychologists make known their commitment to the Ethics Code and take steps to resolve the conflict. If the conflict is unresolvable via such means, psychologists may adhere to the requirements of the law, regulations, or other governing legal authority.

1.03 Conflicts Between Ethics and Organizational Demands
>If the demands of an organization with which psychologists are affiliated or for whom they are working conflict with this Ethics Code, psychologists clarify the nature of the conflict, make known their commitment to the Ethics Code, and to the extent feasible, resolve the conflict in a way that permits adherence to the Ethics Code.

1.04 Informal Resolution of Ethical Violations

When psychologists believe that there may have been an ethical violation by another psychologist, they attempt to resolve the issue by bringing it to the attention of that individual, if an informal resolution appears appropriate and the intervention does not violate any confidentiality rights that may be involved. (See also Standards 1.02, Conflicts Between Ethics and Law, Regulations, or Other Governing Legal Authority, and 1.03, Conflicts Between Ethics and Organizational Demands.)

1.05   Reporting Ethical Violations
If an apparent ethical violation has substantially harmed or is likely to substantially harm a person or organization and is not appropriate for informal resolution under Standard 1.04, Informal Resolution of Ethical Violations, or is not resolved properly in that fashion, psychologists take further action appropriate to the situation. Such action might include referral to state or national committees on professional ethics, to state licensing boards, or to the appropriate institutional authorities. This standard does not apply when an intervention would violate confidentiality rights or when psychologists have been retained to review the work of another psychologist whose professional conduct is in question. (See also Standard 1.02, Conflicts Between Ethics and Law, Regulations, or Other Governing Legal Authority.)

1.06   Cooperating With Ethics Committees
Psychologists cooperate in ethics investigations, proceedings, and resulting requirements of the APA or any affiliated state psychological association to which they belong. In doing so, they address any confidentiality issues. Failure to cooperate is itself an ethics violation. However, making a request for deferment of adjudication of an ethics complaint pending the outcome of litigation does not alone constitute noncooperation.

1.07   Improper Complaints
Psychologists do not file or encourage the filing of ethics complaints that are made with reckless disregard for or willful ignorance of facts that would disprove the allegation.

1.08   Unfair Discrimination Against Complainants and Respondents
Psychologists do not deny persons employment, advancement, admissions to academic or other programs, tenure, or promotion, based solely upon their having made or their being the subject of an ethics

complaint. This does not preclude taking action based upon the outcome of such proceedings or considering other appropriate information.

2. Competence

2.01   Boundaries of Competence

(a) Psychologists provide services, teach, and conduct research with populations and in areas only within the boundaries of their competence, based on their education, training, supervised experience, consultation, study, or professional experience.

(b) Where scientific or professional knowledge in the discipline of psychology establishes that an understanding of factors associated with age, gender, gender identity, race, ethnicity, culture, national origin, religion, sexual orientation, disability, language, or socioeconomic status is essential for effective implementation of their services or research, psychologists have or obtain the training, experience, consultation, or supervision necessary to ensure the competence of their services, or they make appropriate referrals, except as provided in Standard 2.02, Providing Services in Emergencies.

(c) Psychologists planning to provide services, teach, or conduct research involving populations, areas, techniques, or technologies new to them undertake relevant education, training, supervised experience, consultation, or study.

(d) When psychologists are asked to provide services to individuals for whom appropriate mental health services are not available and for which psychologists have not obtained the competence necessary, psychologists with closely related prior training or experience may provide such services in order to ensure that services are not denied if they make a reasonable effort to obtain the competence required by using relevant research, training, consultation, or study.

(e) In those emerging areas in which generally recognized standards for preparatory training do not yet exist, psychologists nevertheless take reasonable steps to ensure the competence of their work and to protect clients/patients, students, supervisees, research participants, organizational clients, and others from harm.

(f) When assuming forensic roles, psychologists are or become reasonably familiar with the judicial or administrative rules governing their roles.

2.02   Providing Services in Emergencies

In emergencies, when psychologists provide services to individuals for whom other mental health services are not available and for which psychologists have not obtained the necessary training, psychologists may provide such services in order to ensure that services are not denied. The services are discontinued as soon as the emergency has ended or appropriate services are available.

2.03   Maintaining Competence

Psychologists undertake ongoing efforts to develop and maintain their competence.

2.04   Bases for Scientific and Professional Judgments

Psychologists' work is based upon established scientific and professional knowledge of the discipline. (See also Standards 2.01e, Boundaries of Competence, and 10.01b, Informed Consent to Therapy.)

2.05   Delegation of Work to Others

Psychologists who delegate work to employees, supervisees, or research or teaching assistants or who use the services of others, such as interpreters, take reasonable steps to (1) avoid delegating such work to persons who have a multiple relationship with those being served that would likely lead to exploitation or loss of objectivity; (2) authorize only those responsibilities that such persons can be expected to perform competently on the basis of their education, training, or experience, either independently or with the level of supervision being provided; and (3) see that such persons perform these services competently. (See also Standards 2.02, Providing Services in Emergencies; 3.05, Multiple Relationships; 4.01, Maintaining Confidentiality; 9.01, Bases for Assessments; 9.02, Use of Assessments; 9.03, Informed Consent in Assessments; and 9.07, Assessment by Unqualified Persons.)

2.06   Personal Problems and Conflicts

(a) Psychologists refrain from initiating an activity when they know or should know that there is a substantial likelihood that their personal problems will prevent them from performing their work-related activities in a competent manner.

(b) When psychologists become aware of personal problems that may interfere with their performing work-related duties adequately, they take appropriate measures, such as obtaining professional consultation or assistance, and determine whether they should limit, suspend, or terminate their work-related duties. (See also Standard 10.10, Terminating Therapy.)

3. Human Relations

3.01   Unfair Discrimination

In their work-related activities, psychologists do not engage in unfair discrimination based on age, gender, gender identity, race, ethnicity, culture, national origin, religion, sexual orientation, disability, socioeconomic status, or any basis proscribed by law.

3.02   Sexual Harassment

Psychologists do not engage in sexual harassment. Sexual harassment is sexual solicitation, physical advances, or verbal or nonverbal conduct that is sexual in nature, that occurs in connection with the psychologist's activities or roles as a psychologist, and that either (1) is unwelcome, is offensive, or creates a hostile workplace or educational environment, and the psychologist knows or is told this or (2) is sufficiently severe or intense to be abusive to a reasonable person in the context. Sexual harassment can consist of a single intense or severe act or of multiple persistent or pervasive acts. (See also Standard 1.08, Unfair Discrimination Against Complainants and Respondents.)

3.03   Other Harassment

Psychologists do not knowingly engage in behavior that is harassing or demeaning to persons with whom they interact in their work based on factors such as those persons' age, gender, gender identity, race, ethnicity, culture, national origin, religion, sexual orientation, disability, language, or socioeconomic status.

3.04   Avoiding Harm

Psychologists take reasonable steps to avoid harming their clients/patients, students, supervisees, research participants, organizational clients, and others with whom they work, and to minimize harm where it is foreseeable and unavoidable.

3.05   Multiple Relationships
(a) A multiple relationship occurs when a psychologist is in a professional role with a person and (1) at the same time is in another role with the same person, (2) at the same time is in a relationship with a person closely associated with or related to the person with whom the psychologist has the professional relationship, or (3) promises to enter into another relationship in the future with the person or a person closely associated with or related to the person.

A psychologist refrains from entering into a multiple relationship if the multiple relationship could reasonably be expected to impair the psychologist's objectivity, competence, or effectiveness in performing his or her functions as a psychologist, or otherwise risks exploitation or harm to the person with whom the professional relationship exists.

Multiple relationships that would not reasonably be expected to cause impairment or risk exploitation or harm are not unethical.

(b) If a psychologist finds that, due to unforeseen factors, a potentially harmful multiple relationship has arisen, the psychologist takes reasonable steps to resolve it with due regard for the best interests of the affected person and maximal compliance with the Ethics Code.

(c) When psychologists are required by law, institutional policy, or extraordinary circumstances to serve in more than one role in judicial or administrative proceedings, at the outset they clarify role expectations and the extent of confidentiality and thereafter as changes occur. (See also Standards 3.04, Avoiding Harm, and 3.07, Third-Party Requests for Services.)

3.06   Conflict of Interest
Psychologists refrain from taking on a professional role when personal, scientific, professional, legal, financial, or other interests or relationships could reasonably be expected to (1) impair their objectivity, competence, or effectiveness in performing their functions as psychologists or (2) expose the person or organization with whom the professional relationship exists to harm or exploitation.

3.07   Third-Party Requests for Services

When psychologists agree to provide services to a person or entity at the request of a third party, psychologists attempt to clarify at the outset of the service the nature of the relationship with all individuals or organizations involved. This clarification includes the role of the psychologist (e.g., therapist, consultant, diagnostician, or expert witness), an identification of who is the client, the probable uses of the services provided or the information obtained, and the fact that there may be limits to confidentiality. (See also Standards 3.05, Multiple Relationships, and 4.02, Discussing the Limits of Confidentiality.)

3.08,   Exploitative Relationships

Psychologists do not exploit persons over whom they have supervisory, evaluative, or other authority such as clients/patients, students, supervisees, research participants, and employees. (See also Standards 3.05, Multiple Relationships; 6.04, Fees and Financial Arrangements; 6.05, Barter With Clients/Patients; 7.07, Sexual Relationships With Students and Supervisees; 10.05, Sexual Intimacies With Current Therapy Clients/Patients; 10.06, Sexual Intimacies With Relatives or Significant Others of Current Therapy Clients/Patients; 10.07, Therapy With Former Sexual Partners; and 10.08, Sexual Intimacies With Former Therapy Clients/Patients.)

3.09   Cooperation With Other Professionals

When indicated and professionally appropriate, psychologists cooperate with other professionals in order to serve their clients/patients effectively and appropriately. (See also Standard 4.05, Disclosures.)

3.10   Informed Consent

(a) When psychologists conduct research or provide assessment, therapy, counseling, or consulting services in person or via electronic transmission or other forms of communication, they obtain the informed consent of the individual or individuals using language that is reasonably understandable to that person or persons except when conducting such activities without consent is mandated by law or governmental regulation or as otherwise provided in this Ethics Code. (See also Standards 8.02, Informed Consent to Research; 9.03, Informed Consent in Assessments; and 10.01, Informed Consent to Therapy.)

(b) For persons who are legally incapable of giving informed consent, psychologists nevertheless (1) provide an appropriate explanation, (2) seek the individual's assent, (3) consider such persons' preferences and best interests, and (4) obtain appropriate permission from a legally authorized person, if such substitute consent is permitted or required by law. When consent by a legally authorized person is not permitted or required by law, psychologists take reasonable steps to protect the individual's rights and welfare.

(c) When psychological services are court ordered or otherwise mandated, psychologists inform the individual of the nature of the anticipated services, including whether the services are court ordered or mandated and any limits of confidentiality, before proceeding.

(d) Psychologists appropriately document written or oral consent, permission, and assent. (See also Standards 8.02, Informed Consent to Research; 9.03, Informed Consent in Assessments; and 10.01, Informed Consent to Therapy.)

3.11   **Psychological Services Delivered To or Through Organizations**
(a) Psychologists delivering services to or through organizations provide information beforehand to clients and when appropriate those directly affected by the services about (1) the nature and objectives of the services, (2) the intended recipients, (3) which of the individuals are clients, (4) the relationship the psychologist will have with each person and the organization, (5) the probable uses of services provided and information obtained, (6) who will have access to the information, and (7) limits of confidentiality. As soon as feasible, they provide information about the results and conclusions of such services to appropriate persons.

(b) If psychologists will be precluded by law or by organizational roles from providing such information to particular individuals or groups, they so inform those individuals or groups at the outset of the service.

3.12   **Interruption of Psychological Services**
Unless otherwise covered by contract, psychologists make reasonable efforts to plan for facilitating services in the event that psychological services are interrupted by factors such as the psychologist's illness, death, unavailability, relocation, or retirement or by the client's/patient's relocation or financial limitations. (See also Standard 6.02c,

Maintenance, Dissemination, and Disposal of Confidential Records of Professional and Scientific Work.)

4. Privacy And Confidentiality

4.01   Maintaining Confidentiality

Psychologists have a primary obligation and take reasonable precautions to protect confidential information obtained through or stored in any medium, recognizing that the extent and limits of confidentiality may be regulated by law or established by institutional rules or professional or scientific relationship. (See also Standard 2.05, Delegation of Work to Others.)

4.02   Discussing the Limits of Confidentiality

(a) Psychologists discuss with persons (including, to the extent feasible, persons who are legally incapable of giving informed consent and their legal representatives) and organizations with whom they establish a scientific or professional relationship (1) the relevant limits of confidentiality and (2) the foreseeable uses of the information generated through their psychological activities. (See also Standard 3.10, Informed Consent.)

(b) Unless it is not feasible or is contraindicated, the discussion of confidentiality occurs at the outset of the relationship and thereafter as new circumstances may warrant.

(c) Psychologists who offer services, products, or information via electronic transmission inform clients/patients of the risks to privacy and limits of confidentiality.

4.03   Recording

Before recording the voices or images of individuals to whom they provide services, psychologists obtain permission from all such persons or their legal representatives. (See also Standards 8.03, Informed Consent for Recording Voices and Images in Research; 8.05, Dispensing With Informed Consent for Research; and 8.07, Deception in Research.)

4.04   Minimizing Intrusions on Privacy

(a) Psychologists include in written and oral reports and consultations, only information germane to the purpose for which the communication is made.

(b) Psychologists discuss confidential information obtained in their work only for appropriate scientific or professional purposes and only with persons clearly concerned with such matters.

4.05   Disclosures
(a) Psychologists may disclose confidential information with the appropriate consent of the organizational client, the individual client/patient, or another legally authorized person on behalf of the client/patient unless prohibited by law.

(b) Psychologists disclose confidential information without the consent of the individual only as mandated by law, or where permitted by law for a valid purpose such as to (1) provide needed professional services; (2) obtain appropriate professional consultations; (3) protect the client/patient, psychologist, or others from harm; or (4) obtain payment for services from a client/patient, in which instance disclosure is limited to the minimum that is necessary to achieve the purpose. (See also Standard 6.04e, Fees and Financial Arrangements.)

4.06   Consultations
When consulting with colleagues, (1) psychologists do not disclose confidential information that reasonably could lead to the identification of a client/patient, research participant, or other person or organization with whom they have a confidential relationship unless they have obtained the prior consent of the person or organization or the disclosure cannot be avoided, and (2) they disclose information only to the extent necessary to achieve the purposes of the consultation. (See also Standard 4.01, Maintaining Confidentiality.)

4.07   Use of Confidential Information for Didactic or Other Purposes
Psychologists do not disclose in their writings, lectures, or other public media, confidential, personally identifiable information concerning their clients/patients, students, research participants, organizational clients, or other recipients of their services that they obtained during the course of their work, unless (1) they take reasonable steps to disguise the person or organization, (2) the person or organization has consented in writing, or (3) there is legal authorization for doing so.

5. Advertising and Other Public Statements

5.01   **Avoidance of False or Deceptive Statements**
(a) Public statements include but are not limited to paid or unpaid advertising, product endorsements, grant applications, licensing applications, other credentialing applications, brochures, printed matter, directory listings, personal resumes or curricula vitae, or comments for use in media such as print or electronic transmission, statements in legal proceedings, lectures and public oral presentations, and published materials. Psychologists do not knowingly make public statements that are false, deceptive, or fraudulent concerning their research, practice, or other work activities or those of persons or organizations with which they are affiliated.

(b) Psychologists do not make false, deceptive, or fraudulent statements concerning (1) their training, experience, or competence; (2) their academic degrees; (3) their credentials; (4) their institutional or association affiliations; (5) their services; (6) the scientific or clinical basis for, or results or degree of success of, their services; (7) their fees; or (8) their publications or research findings.

(c) Psychologists claim degrees as credentials for their health services only if those degrees (1) were earned from a regionally accredited educational institution or (2) were the basis for psychology licensure by the state in which they practice.

5.02   **Statements by Others**
(a) Psychologists who engage others to create or place public statements that promote their professional practice, products, or activities retain professional responsibility for such statements.

(b) Psychologists do not compensate employees of press, radio, television, or other communication media in return for publicity in a news item. (See also Standard 1.01, Misuse of Psychologists' Work.)

(c) A paid advertisement relating to psychologists' activities must be identified or clearly recognizable as such.

5.03   **Descriptions of Workshops and Non-Degree-Granting Educational Programs**

To the degree to which they exercise control, psychologists responsible for announcements, catalogs, brochures, or advertisements describing workshops, seminars, or other non-degree-granting educational programs ensure that they accurately describe the audience for which the program is intended, the educational objectives, the presenters, and the fees involved.

5.04   Media Presentations
When psychologists provide public advice or comment via print, Internet, or other electronic transmission, they take precautions to ensure that statements (1) are based on their professional knowledge, training, or experience in accord with appropriate psychological literature and practice; (2) are otherwise consistent with this Ethics Code; and (3) do not indicate that a professional relationship has been established with the recipient. (See also Standard 2.04, Bases for Scientific and Professional Judgments.)

5.05   Testimonials
Psychologists do not solicit testimonials from current therapy clients/patients or other persons who because of their particular circumstances are vulnerable to undue influence.

5.06   In-Person Solicitation
Psychologists do not engage, directly or through agents, in uninvited in-person solicitation of business from actual or potential therapy clients/patients or other persons who because of their particular circumstances are vulnerable to undue influence. However, this prohibition does not preclude (1) attempting to implement appropriate collateral contacts for the purpose of benefiting an already engaged therapy client/patient or (2) providing disaster or community outreach services.

6. Record Keeping and Fees

6.01   Documentation of Professional and Scientific Work and Maintenance of Records
Psychologists create, and to the extent the records are under their control, maintain, disseminate, store, retain, and dispose of records and data relating to their professional and scientific work in order to (1) facilitate provision of services later by them or by other professionals, (2) allow for replication of research design and analyses, (3) meet

institutional requirements, (4) ensure accuracy of billing and payments, and (5) ensure compliance with law. (See also Standard 4.01, Maintaining Confidentiality.)

6.02   **Maintenance, Dissemination, and Disposal of Confidential Records of Professional and Scientific Work**
(a) Psychologists maintain confidentiality in creating, storing, accessing, transferring, and disposing of records under their control, whether these are written, automated, or in any other medium. (See also Standards 4.01, Maintaining Confidentiality, and 6.01, Documentation of Professional and Scientific Work and Maintenance of Records.)

b) If confidential information concerning recipients of psychological services is entered into databases or systems of records available to persons whose access has not been consented to by the recipient, psychologists use coding or other techniques to avoid the inclusion of personal identifiers.

(c) Psychologists make plans in advance to facilitate the appropriate transfer and to protect the confidentiality of records and data in the event of psychologists' withdrawal from positions or practice. (See also Standards 3.12, Interruption of Psychological Services, and 10.09, Interruption of Therapy.)

6.03   **Withholding Records for Nonpayment**
Psychologists may not withhold records under their control that are requested and needed for a client's/patient's emergency treatment solely because payment has not been received.

6.04   **Fees and Financial Arrangements**
(a) As early as is feasible in a professional or scientific relationship, psychologists and recipients of psychological services reach an agreement specifying compensation and billing arrangements.

(b) Psychologists' fee practices are consistent with law.

(c) Psychologists do not misrepresent their fees.

(d) If limitations to services can be anticipated because of limitations in financing, this is discussed with the recipient of services as early as is feasible. (See also Standards 10.09, Interruption of Therapy, and 10.10, Terminating Therapy.)

(e) If the recipient of services does not pay for services as agreed, and if psychologists intend to use collection agencies or legal measures to collect the fees, psychologists first inform the person that such measures will be taken and provide that person an opportunity to make prompt payment. (See also Standards 4.05, Disclosures; 6.03, Withholding Records for Nonpayment; and 10.01, Informed Consent to Therapy.)

6.05   Barter With Clients/Patients
Barter is the acceptance of goods, services, or other nonmonetary remuneration from clients/patients in return for psychological services. Psychologists may barter only if (1) it is not clinically contraindicated, and (2) the resulting arrangement is not exploitative. (See also Standards 3.05, Multiple Relationships, and 6.04, Fees and Financial Arrangements.)

6.06   Accuracy in Reports to Payors and Funding Sources
In their reports to payors for services or sources of research funding, psychologists take reasonable steps to ensure the accurate reporting of the nature of the service provided or research conducted, the fees, charges, or payments, and where applicable, the identity of the provider, the findings, and the diagnosis. (See also Standards 4.01, Maintaining Confidentiality; 4.04, Minimizing Intrusions on Privacy; and 4.05, Disclosures.)

6.07   Referrals and Fees
When psychologists pay, receive payment from, or divide fees with another professional, other than in an employer-employee relationship, the payment to each is based on the services provided (clinical, consultative, administrative, or other) and is not based on the referral itself. (See also Standard 3.09, Cooperation With Other Professionals.)

7. Education and Training

7.01   Design of Education and Training Programs
Psychologists responsible for education and training programs take reasonable steps to ensure that the programs are designed to provide the appropriate knowledge and proper experiences, and to meet the

requirements for licensure, certification, or other goals for which claims are made by the program. (See also Standard 5.03, Descriptions of Workshops and Non-Degree-Granting Educational Programs.)

7.02   Descriptions of Education and Training Programs
Psychologists responsible for education and training programs take reasonable steps to ensure that there is a current and accurate description of the program content (including participation in required course – or program-related counseling, psychotherapy, experiential groups, consulting projects, or community service), training goals and objectives, stipends and benefits, and requirements that must be met for satisfactory completion of the program. This information must be made readily available to all interested parties.

7.03   Accuracy in Teaching
(a) Psychologists take reasonable steps to ensure that course syllabi are accurate regarding the subject matter to be covered, bases for evaluating progress, and the nature of course experiences. This standard does not preclude an instructor from modifying course content or requirements when the instructor considers it pedagogically necessary or desirable, so long as students are made aware of these modifications in a manner that enables them to fulfill course requirements. (See also Standard 5.01, Avoidance of False or Deceptive Statements.)

(b) When engaged in teaching or training, psychologists present psychological information accurately. (See also Standard 2.03, Maintaining Competence.)

7.04   Student Disclosure of Personal Information
Psychologists do not require students or supervisees to disclose personal information in course – or program-related activities, either orally or in writing, regarding sexual history, history of abuse and neglect, psychological treatment, and relationships with parents, peers, and spouses or significant others except if (1) the program or training facility has clearly identified this requirement in its admissions and program materials or (2) the information is necessary to evaluate or obtain assistance for students whose personal problems could reasonably be judged to be preventing them from performing their training – or professionally related activities in a competent manner or posing a threat to the students or others.

7.05   **Mandatory Individual or Group Therapy**
(a) When individual or group therapy is a program or course requirement, psychologists responsible for that program allow students in undergraduate and graduate programs the option of selecting such therapy from practitioners unaffiliated with the program. (See also Standard 7.02, Descriptions of Education and Training Programs.)

(b) Faculty who are or are likely to be responsible for evaluating students' academic performance do not themselves provide that therapy. (See also Standard 3.05, Multiple Relationships.)

7.06   **Assessing Student and Supervisee Performance**
(a) In academic and supervisory relationships, psychologists establish a timely and specific process for providing feedback to students and supervisees. Information regarding the process is provided to the student at the beginning of supervision.

(b) Psychologists evaluate students and supervisees on the basis of their actual performance on relevant and established program requirements.

7.07   **Sexual Relationships With Students and Supervisees**
Psychologists do not engage in sexual relationships with students or supervisees who are in their department, agency, or training center or over whom psychologists have or are likely to have evaluative authority. (See also Standard 3.05, Multiple Relationships.)

8. Research and Publication

8.01   **Institutional Approval**
When institutional approval is required, psychologists provide accurate information about their research proposals and obtain approval prior to conducting the research. They conduct the research in accordance with the approved research protocol.

8.02   **Informed Consent to Research**
(a) When obtaining informed consent as required in Standard 3.10, Informed Consent, psychologists inform participants about (1) the purpose of the research, expected duration, and procedures; (2) their right to decline to participate and to withdraw from the research once

participation has begun; (3) the foreseeable consequences of declining or withdrawing; (4) reasonably foreseeable factors that may be expected to influence their willingness to participate such as potential risks, discomfort, or adverse effects; (5) any prospective research benefits; (6) limits of confidentiality; (7) incentives for participation; and (8) whom to contact for questions about the research and research participants' rights. They provide opportunity for the prospective participants to ask questions and receive answers. (See also Standards 8.03, Informed Consent for Recording Voices and Images in Research; 8.05, Dispensing With Informed Consent for Research; and 8.07, Deception in Research.)

(b) Psychologists conducting intervention research involving the use of experimental treatments clarify to participants at the outset of the research (1) the experimental nature of the treatment; (2) the services that will or will not be available to the control group(s) if appropriate; (3) the means by which assignment to treatment and control groups will be made; (4) available treatment alternatives if an individual does not wish to participate in the research or wishes to withdraw once a study has begun; and (5) compensation for or monetary costs of participating including, if appropriate, whether reimbursement from the participant or a third-party payor will be sought. (See also Standard 8.02a, Informed Consent to Research.)

8.03   **Informed Consent for Recording Voices and Images in Research**
Psychologists obtain informed consent from research participants prior to recording their voices or images for data collection unless (1) the research consists solely of naturalistic observations in public places, and it is not anticipated that the recording will be used in a manner that could cause personal identification or harm, or (2) the research design includes deception, and consent for the use of the recording is obtained during debriefing. (See also Standard 8.07, Deception in Research.)

8.04   **Client/Patient, Student, and Subordinate Research Participants**
(a) When psychologists conduct research with clients/patients, students, or subordinates as participants, psychologists take steps to protect the prospective participants from adverse consequences of declining or withdrawing from participation.

(b) When research participation is a course requirement or an opportunity for extra credit, the prospective participant is given the choice of equitable alternative activities.

8.05   Dispensing With Informed Consent for Research
Psychologists may dispense with informed consent only (1) where research would not reasonably be assumed to create distress or harm and involves (a) the study of normal educational practices, curricula, or classroom management methods conducted in educational settings; (b) only anonymous questionnaires, naturalistic observations, or archival research for which disclosure of responses would not place participants at risk of criminal or civil liability or damage their financial standing, employability, or reputation, and confidentiality is protected; or (c) the study of factors related to job or organization effectiveness conducted in organizational settings for which there is no risk to participants' employability, and confidentiality is protected or (2) where otherwise permitted by law or federal or institutional regulations.

8.06   Offering Inducements for Research Participation
(a) Psychologists make reasonable efforts to avoid offering excessive or inappropriate financial or other inducements for research participation when such inducements are likely to coerce participation.

(b) When offering professional services as an inducement for research participation, psychologists clarify the nature of the services, as well as the risks, obligations, and limitations. (See also Standard 6.05, Barter With Clients/Patients.)

8.07   Deception in Research
(a) Psychologists do not conduct a study involving deception unless they have determined that the use of deceptive techniques is justified by the study's significant prospective scientific, educational, or applied value and that effective nondeceptive alternative procedures are not feasible.

(b) Psychologists do not deceive prospective participants about research that is reasonably expected to cause physical pain or severe emotional distress.

(c) Psychologists explain any deception that is an integral feature of the design and conduct of an experiment to participants as early as is feasible, preferably at the conclusion of their participation, but no later than at the conclusion of the data collection, and permit participants to withdraw their data. (See also Standard 8.08, Debriefing.)

8.08   Debriefing

(a) Psychologists provide a prompt opportunity for participants to obtain appropriate information about the nature, results, and conclusions of the research, and they take reasonable steps to correct any misconceptions that participants may have of which the psychologists are aware.

(b) If scientific or humane values justify delaying or withholding this information, psychologists take reasonable measures to reduce the risk of harm.

(c) When psychologists become aware that research procedures have harmed a participant, they take reasonable steps to minimize the harm.

8.09   Humane Care and Use of Animals in Research

(a) Psychologists acquire, care for, use, and dispose of animals in compliance with current federal, state, and local laws and regulations, and with professional standards.

(b) Psychologists trained in research methods and experienced in the care of laboratory animals supervise all procedures involving animals and are responsible for ensuring appropriate consideration of their comfort, health, and humane treatment.

(c) Psychologists ensure that all individuals under their supervision who are using animals have received instruction in research methods and in the care, maintenance, and handling of the species being used, to the extent appropriate to their role. (See also Standard 2.05, Delegation of Work to Others.)

(d) Psychologists make reasonable efforts to minimize the discomfort, infection, illness, and pain of animal subjects.

(e) Psychologists use a procedure subjecting animals to pain, stress, or privation only when an alternative procedure is unavailable and the goal is justified by its prospective scientific, educational, or applied value.

(f) Psychologists perform surgical procedures under appropriate anesthesia and follow techniques to avoid infection and minimize pain during and after surgery.

(g) When it is appropriate that an animal's life be terminated, psychologists proceed rapidly, with an effort to minimize pain and in accordance with accepted procedures.

8.10   **Reporting Research Results**
(a) Psychologists do not fabricate data. (See also Standard 5.01a, Avoidance of False or Deceptive Statements.)

(b) If psychologists discover significant errors in their published data, they take reasonable steps to correct such errors in a correction, retraction, erratum, or other appropriate publication means.

8.11   **Plagiarism**
Psychologists do not present portions of another's work or data as their own, even if the other work or data source is cited occasionally.

8.12   **Publication Credit**
(a) Psychologists take responsibility and credit, including authorship credit, only for work they have actually performed or to which they have substantially contributed. (See also Standard 8.12b, Publication Credit.)

(b) Principal authorship and other publication credits accurately reflect the relative scientific or professional contributions of the individuals involved, regardless of their relative status. Mere possession of an institutional position, such as department chair, does not justify authorship credit. Minor contributions to the research or to the writing for publications are acknowledged appropriately, such as in footnotes or in an introductory statement.

(c) Except under exceptional circumstances, a student is listed as principal author on any multiple-authored article that is substantially based on the student's doctoral dissertation. Faculty advisors discuss publication credit with students as early as feasible and throughout the research and publication process as appropriate. (See also Standard 8.12b, Publication Credit.)

8.13   Duplicate Publication of Data

Psychologists do not publish, as original data, data that have been previously published. This does not preclude republishing data when they are accompanied by proper acknowledgment.

8.14   Sharing Research Data for Verification

(a) After research results are published, psychologists do not withhold the data on which their conclusions are based from other competent professionals who seek to verify the substantive claims through reanalysis and who intend to use such data only for that purpose, provided that the confidentiality of the participants can be protected and unless legal rights concerning proprietary data preclude their release. This does not preclude psychologists from requiring that such individuals or groups be responsible for costs associated with the provision of such information.

(b) Psychologists who request data from other psychologists to verify the substantive claims through reanalysis may use shared data only for the declared purpose. Requesting psychologists obtain prior written agreement for all other uses of the data.

8.15   Reviewers

Psychologists who review material submitted for presentation, publication, grant, or research proposal review respect the confidentiality of and the proprietary rights in such information of those who submitted it.

9. Assessment

9.01   Bases for Assessments

(a) Psychologists base the opinions contained in their recommendations, reports, and diagnostic or evaluative statements, including forensic testimony, on information and techniques sufficient to substantiate their findings. (See also Standard 2.04, Bases for Scientific and Professional Judgments.)

(b) Except as noted in 9.01c, psychologists provide opinions of the psychological characteristics of individuals only after they have conducted an examination of the individuals adequate to support their statements or conclusions. When, despite reasonable efforts, such an examination is not practical, psychologists document the efforts they made and the result of those efforts, clarify the probable impact of their limited information on the reliability and validity of their opinions, and appropriately limit the nature and extent of their conclusions or recommendations. (See also Standards 2.01, Boundaries of Competence, and 9.06, Interpreting Assessment Results.)

(c) When psychologists conduct a record review or provide consultation or supervision and an individual examination is not warranted or necessary for the opinion, psychologists explain this and the sources of information on which they based their conclusions and recommendations.

9.02   **Use of Assessments**
(a) Psychologists administer, adapt, score, interpret, or use assessment techniques, interviews, tests, or instruments in a manner and for purposes that are appropriate in light of the research on or evidence of the usefulness and proper application of the techniques.

(b) Psychologists use assessment instruments whose validity and reliability have been established for use with members of the population tested. When such validity or reliability has not been established, psychologists describe the strengths and limitations of test results and interpretation.

(c) Psychologists use assessment methods that are appropriate to an individual's language preference and competence, unless the use of an alternative language is relevant to the assessment issues.

9.03   **Informed Consent in Assessments**
(a) Psychologists obtain informed consent for assessments, evaluations, or diagnostic services, as described in Standard 3.10, Informed Consent, except when (1) testing is mandated by law or governmental regulations; (2) informed consent is implied because testing is conducted as a routine educational, institutional, or organizational activity (e.g., when participants voluntarily agree to assessment when applying for a job); or (3) one purpose of the testing is to evaluate decisional capacity. Informed consent includes an explanation of the nature and purpose of the assessment, fees, involvement of third parties, and limits of confidentiality and sufficient opportunity for the client/patient to ask questions and receive answers.

(b) Psychologists inform persons with questionable capacity to consent or for whom testing is mandated by law or governmental regulations about the nature and purpose of the proposed assessment services, using language that is reasonably understandable to the person being assessed.

(c) Psychologists using the services of an interpreter obtain informed consent from the client/patient to use that interpreter, ensure that confidentiality of test results and test security are maintained, and include in their recommendations, reports, and diagnostic or evaluative statements, including forensic testimony, discussion of any limitations on the data obtained. (See also Standards 2.05, Delegation of Work to Others; 4.01, Maintaining Confidentiality; 9.01, Bases for Assessments; 9.06, Interpreting Assessment Results; and 9.07, Assessment by Unqualified Persons.)

9.04   Release of Test Data
(a) The term test data refers to raw and scaled scores, client/patient responses to test questions or stimuli, and psychologists' notes and recordings concerning client/patient statements and behavior during an examination. Those portions of test materials that include client/patient responses are included in the definition of test data. Pursuant to a client/patient release, psychologists provide test data to the client/patient or other persons identified in the release. Psychologists may refrain from releasing test data to protect a client/patient or others from substantial harm or misuse or misrepresentation of the data or the test, recognizing that in many instances release of confidential information under these circumstances is regulated by law. (See also Standard 9.11, Maintaining Test Security.)

(b) In the absence of a client/patient release, psychologists provide test data only as required by law or court order.

9.05   Test Construction
Psychologists who develop tests and other assessment techniques use appropriate psychometric procedures and current scientific or professional knowledge for test design, standardization, validation, reduction or elimination of bias, and recommendations for use.

9.06   Interpreting Assessment Results

When interpreting assessment results, including automated interpretations, psychologists take into account the purpose of the assessment as well as the various test factors, test-taking abilities, and other characteristics of the person being assessed, such as situational, personal, linguistic, and cultural differences, that might affect psychologists' judgments or reduce the accuracy of their interpretations. They indicate any significant limitations of their interpretations. (See also Standards 2.01b and c, Boundaries of Competence, and 3.01, Unfair Discrimination.)

9.07   **Assessment by Unqualified Persons**
Psychologists do not promote the use of psychological assessment techniques by unqualified persons, except when such use is conducted for training purposes with appropriate supervision. (See also Standard 2.05, Delegation of Work to Others.)

9.08   **Obsolete Tests and Outdated Test Results**
(a) Psychologists do not base their assessment or intervention decisions or recommendations on data or test results that are outdated for the current purpose.

(b) Psychologists do not base such decisions or recommendations on tests and measures that are obsolete and not useful for the current purpose.

9.09   **Test Scoring and Interpretation Services**
(a) Psychologists who offer assessment or scoring services to other professionals accurately describe the purpose, norms, validity, reliability, and applications of the procedures and any special qualifications applicable to their use.

(b) Psychologists select scoring and interpretation services (including automated services) on the basis of evidence of the validity of the program and procedures as well as on other appropriate considerations. (See also Standard 2.01b and c, Boundaries of Competence.)

(c) Psychologists retain responsibility for the appropriate application, interpretation, and use of assessment instruments, whether they score and interpret such tests themselves or use automated or other services.

9.10   **Explaining Assessment Results**

Regardless of whether the scoring and interpretation are done by psychologists, by employees or assistants, or by automated or other outside services, psychologists take reasonable steps to ensure that explanations of results are given to the individual or designated representative unless the nature of the relationship precludes provision of an explanation of results (such as in some organizational consulting, preemployment or security screenings, and forensic evaluations), and this fact has been clearly explained to the person being assessed in advance.

9.11.   **Maintaining Test Security**

The term test materials refers to manuals, instruments, protocols, and test questions or stimuli and does not include test data as defined in Standard 9.04, Release of Test Data. Psychologists make reasonable efforts to maintain the integrity and security of test materials and other assessment techniques consistent with law and contractual obligations, and in a manner that permits adherence to this Ethics Code.

10. Therapy

10.01   **Informed Consent to Therapy**

(a) When obtaining informed consent to therapy as required in Standard 3.10, Informed Consent, psychologists inform clients/patients as early as is feasible in the therapeutic relationship about the nature and anticipated course of therapy, fees, involvement of third parties, and limits of confidentiality and provide sufficient opportunity for the client/patient to ask questions and receive answers. (See also Standards 4.02, Discussing the Limits of Confidentiality, and 6.04, Fees and Financial Arrangements.)

(b) When obtaining informed consent for treatment for which generally recognized techniques and procedures have not been established, psychologists inform their clients/patients of the developing nature of the treatment, the potential risks involved, alternative treatments that may be available, and the voluntary nature of their participation. (See also Standards 2.01e, Boundaries of Competence, and 3.10, Informed Consent.)

(c) When the therapist is a trainee and the legal responsibility for the treatment provided resides with the supervisor, the client/patient, as part of the informed consent procedure, is informed that the therapist is in training and is being supervised and is given the name of the supervisor.

10.02   **Therapy Involving Couples or Families**
(a) When psychologists agree to provide services to several persons who have a relationship (such as spouses, significant others, or parents and children), they take reasonable steps to clarify at the outset (1) which of the individuals are clients/patients and (2) the relationship the psychologist will have with each person. This clarification includes the psychologist's role and the probable uses of the services provided or the information obtained. (See also Standard 4.02, Discussing the Limits of Confidentiality.)

(b) If it becomes apparent that psychologists may be called on to perform potentially conflicting roles (such as family therapist and then witness for one party in divorce proceedings), psychologists take reasonable steps to clarify and modify, or withdraw from, roles appropriately. (See also Standard 3.05c, Multiple Relationships.)

10.03   **Group Therapy**
When psychologists provide services to several persons in a group setting, they describe at the outset the roles and responsibilities of all parties and the limits of confidentiality.

10.04   **Providing Therapy to Those Served by Others**
In deciding whether to offer or provide services to those already receiving mental health services elsewhere, psychologists carefully consider the treatment issues and the potential client's/patient's welfare. Psychologists discuss these issues with the client/patient or another legally authorized person on behalf of the client/patient in order to minimize the risk of confusion and conflict, consult with the other service providers when appropriate, and proceed with caution and sensitivity to the therapeutic issues.

10.05   **Sexual Intimacies With Current Therapy Clients/Patients**
Psychologists do not engage in sexual intimacies with current therapy clients/patients.

10.06   **Sexual Intimacies With Relatives or Significant Others of Current Therapy Clients/Patients**

Psychologists do not engage in sexual intimacies with individuals they know to be close relatives, guardians, or significant others of current clients/patients. Psychologists do not terminate therapy to circumvent this standard.

10.07   Therapy With Former Sexual Partners
Psychologists do not accept as therapy clients/patients persons with whom they have engaged in sexual intimacies.

10.08   Sexual Intimacies With Former Therapy Clients/Patients
(a) Psychologists do not engage in sexual intimacies with former clients/patients for at least two years after cessation or termination of therapy.

(b) Psychologists do not engage in sexual intimacies with former clients/patients even after a two-year interval except in the most unusual circumstances. Psychologists who engage in such activity after the two years following cessation or termination of therapy and of having no sexual contact with the former client/patient bear the burden of demonstrating that there has been no exploitation, in light of all relevant factors, including (1) the amount of time that has passed since therapy terminated; (2) the nature, duration, and intensity of the therapy; (3) the circumstances of termination; (4) the client's/patient's personal history; (5) the client's/patient's current mental status; (6) the likelihood of adverse impact on the client/patient; and (7) any statements or actions made by the therapist during the course of therapy suggesting or inviting the possibility of a posttermination sexual or romantic relationship with the client/patient. (See also Standard 3.05, Multiple Relationships.)

10.09   Interruption of Therapy
When entering into employment or contractual relationships, psychologists make reasonable efforts to provide for orderly and appropriate resolution of responsibility for client/patient care in the event that the employment or contractual relationship ends, with paramount consideration given to the welfare of the client/patient. (See also Standard 3.12, Interruption of Psychological Services.)

10.10   Terminating Therapy

(a) Psychologists terminate therapy when it becomes reasonably clear that the client/patient no longer needs the service, is not likely to benefit, or is being harmed by continued service.

(b) Psychologists may terminate therapy when threatened or otherwise endangered by the client/patient or another person with whom the client/patient has a relationship.

(c) Except where precluded by the actions of clients/patients or third-party payors, prior to termination psychologists provide pretermination counseling and suggest alternative service providers as appropriate.

HISTORY AND EFFECTIVE DATE

This version of the APA Ethics Code was adopted by the American Psychological Association's Council of Representatives during its meeting, August 21, 2002, and is effective beginning June 1, 2003. Inquiries concerning the substance or interpretation of the APA Ethics Code should be addressed to the Director, Office of Ethics, American Psychological Association, 750 First Street, NE, Washington, DC 20002-4242. The Ethics Code and information regarding the Code can be found on the APA web site, http://www.apa.org/ethics. The standards in this Ethics Code will be used to adjudicate complaints brought concerning alleged conduct occurring on or after the effective date. Complaints regarding conduct occurring prior to the effective date will be adjudicated on the basis of the version of the Ethics Code that was in effect at the time the conduct occurred.

The APA has previously published its Ethics Code as follows:

American Psychological Association. (1953). Ethical standards of psychologists. Washington, DC: Author.

American Psychological Association. (1959). Ethical standards of psychologists. American Psychologist, 14, 279-282.

American Psychological Association. (1963). Ethical standards of psychologists. American Psychologist, 18, 56-60.

American Psychological Association. (1968). Ethical standards of psychologists. American Psychologist, 23, 357-361.

American Psychological Association. (1977, March). Ethical standards of psychologists. APA Monitor, 22-23.

American Psychological Association. (1979). Ethical standards of psychologists. Washington, DC: Author.

American Psychological Association. (1981). Ethical principles of psychologists. American Psychologist, 36, 633-638.

American Psychological Association. (1990). Ethical principles of psychologists (Amended June 2, 1989). American Psychologist, 45, 390-395.

American Psychological Association. (1992). Ethical principles of psychologists and code of conduct. American Psychologist, 47, 1597-1611.

Request copies of the APA's Ethical Principles of Psychologists and Code of Conduct from the APA Order Department, 750 First Street, NE, Washington, DC 20002-4242, or phone (202) 336-5510.

**Appendix A-3
American School Counselor Association**

Ethical Standards for School Counselors
Revised June 25, 1998

Preamble

The American School Counselor Association (ASCA) is a professional organization whose members have a unique and distinctive preparation, grounded in the behavioral sciences, with training in clinical skills adapted to the school setting. The school counselor assists in the growth and development of each individual and uses his or her highly specialized skills to protect the interests of the counselee within the structure of the school system. School counselors subscribe to the following basic tenets of the counseling process from which professional responsibilities are derived:

- Each person has the right to respect and dignity as a human being and to counseling services without prejudice as to person, character, belief, or practice regardless of age, color, disability, ethnic group, gender, race, religion, sexual orientation, marital status, or socioeconomic status.
- Each person has the right to self-direction and self-development.
- Each person has the right of choice and the responsibility for goals reached.
- Each person has the right to privacy and thereby the right to expect the counselor-counselee relationship to comply with all laws, policies, and ethical standards pertaining to confidentiality.

In this document, ASCA specifies the principles of ethical behavior necessary to regulate and maintain the high standards of integrity, leadership, and professionalism among its members. The Ethical Standards for School Counselors were developed to clarify the nature of ethical responsibilities held in common by school counseling professionals. The purposes of this document are to:

- Serve as a guide for the ethical practices of all professional school counselors regardless of level, area, population served, or membership in this professional Association;
- Provide benchmarks for both self-appraisal and peer evaluations regarding counselor responsibilities to counselees, parents, colleagues

and professional associates, schools, and communities, as well as to one's self and the counseling profession; and

- Inform those served by the school counselor of acceptable counselor practices and expected professional behavior.

A.1. Responsibilities to Students

The professional school counselor:

a. Has a primary obligation to the counselee who is to be treated with respect as a unique individual.

b. Is concerned with the educational, career, emotional, and behavioral needs and encourages the maximum development of each counselee.

c. Refrains from consciously encouraging the counselee's acceptance of values, lifestyles, plans, decisions, and beliefs that represent the counselor's personal orientation.

d. Is responsible for keeping informed of laws, regulations, and policies relating to counselees and strives to ensure that the rights of counselees are adequately provided for and protected.

A.2. Confidentiality

The professional school counselor:

a. Informs the counselee of the purposes, goals, techniques, and rules of procedure under which she/he may receive counseling at or before the time when the counseling relationship is entered. Disclosure notice includes confidentiality issues such as the possible necessity for consulting with other professionals, privileged communication, and legal or authoritative restraints. The meaning and limits of confidentiality are clearly defined to counselees through a written and shared disclosure statement.

b. Keeps information confidential unless disclosure is required to prevent clear and imminent danger to the counselee or others or when legal requirements demand that confidential information be revealed. Counselors will consult with other professionals when in doubt as to the validity of an exception.

c. Discloses information to an identified third party who, by her or his relationship with the counselee, is at a high risk of contracting a disease that is commonly known to be communicable and fatal. Prior to disclosure, the counselor will ascertain that the counselee has not already informed the third party about his or her disease and he/she is not intending to inform the third party in the immediate future.

d. Requests of the court that disclosure not be required when the release of confidential information without a counselee's permission may lead to potential harm to the counselee.

e. Protects the confidentiality of counselee's records and releases personal data only according to prescribed laws and school policies. Student information maintained in computers is treated with the same care as traditional student records.

f. Protects the confidentiality of information received in the counseling relationship as specified by federal and state laws, written policies, and applicable ethical standards. Such information is only to be revealed to others with the informed consent of the counselee, consistent with the counselor's ethical obligation. In a group setting, the counselor sets a high norm of confidentiality and stresses its importance, yet clearly states that confidentiality in group counseling cannot be guaranteed.

A.3. Counseling Plans

The professional school counselor:

works jointly with the counselee in developing integrated and effective counseling plans, consistent with both the abilities and circumstances of the counselee and counselor. Such plans will be regularly reviewed to ensure continued viability and effectiveness, respecting the counselee's freedom of choice.

A.4. Dual Relationships

The professional school counselor:

avoids dual relationships which might impair her or his objectivity and increase the risk of harm to the client (e.g., counseling one's family members, close friends, or associates). If a dual relationship is unavoidable, the counselor is responsible for taking action to eliminate or reduce the potential for harm. Such safeguards might include informed consent, consultation, supervision, and documentation.

A.5. Appropriate Referrals

The professional school counselor:

makes referrals when necessary or appropriate to outside resources. Appropriate referral necessitates knowledge of available resources and making proper plans for transitions with minimal interruption of services. Counselees retain the right to discontinue the counseling relationship at any time.

A.6. Group Work

The professional school counselor:

screens prospective group members and maintains an awareness of participants' needs and goals in relation to the goals of the group. The counselor takes reasonable precautions to protect members from physical and psychological harm resulting from interaction within the group.

A 7. Danger to Self or Others

The professional school counselor:

informs appropriate authorities when the counselee's condition indicates a clear and imminent danger to the counselee or others. This is to be done after careful deliberation and, where possible, after consultation with other counseling professionals. The counselor informs the counselee of actions to be taken so as to minimize his or her confusion and to clarify counselee and counselor expectations.

A.8. Student Records

The professional school counselor:

maintains and secures records necessary for rendering professional services to the counselee as required by laws, regulations, institutional procedures, and confidentiality guidelines.

A.9. Evaluation, Assessment, and Interpretation

The professional school counselor:

a. Adheres to all professional standards regarding selecting, administering, and interpreting assessment measures. The counselor recognizes that computer-based testing programs require specific training in administration, scoring, and interpretation which may differ from that required in more traditional assessments.

b. Provides explanations of the nature, purposes, and results of assessment/evaluation measures in language the counselee(s) can understand.

c. Does not misuse assessment results and interpretations and takes reasonable steps to prevent others from misusing the information.

d. Uses caution when utilizing assessment techniques, making evaluations, and interpreting the performance of populations not represented in the norm group on which an instrument is standardized.

A.10. Computer Technology

The professional school counselor:

a. Promotes the benefits of appropriate computer applications and clarifies the limitations of computer technology. The counselor ensures that: (1) computer applications are appropriate for the individual needs of the counselee; (2) the counselee understands how to use the application; and (3) follow-up counseling assistance is provided. Members of under represented groups are assured equal access to computer technologies and are assured the absence of discriminatory information and values in computer applications.

b. Counselors who communicate with counselees via internet should follow the NBCC Standards for Web Counseling.

A.11. Peer Helper Programs

The professional school counselor:

has unique responsibilities when working with peer helper programs. The school counselor is responsible for the welfare of counselees participating in peer programs under her or his direction. School counselors who function in training and supervisory capacities are referred to the preparation and supervision standards of professional counselor associations.

B. Responsibilities to Parents

B.1. Parent Rights and Responsibilities

The professional school counselor:

a. Respects the inherent rights and responsibilities of parents for their children and endeavors to establish, as appropriate, a collaborative relationship with parents to facilitate the counselee's maximum development.

b. Adheres to laws and local guidelines when assisting parents experiencing family difficulties that interfere with the counselee's effectiveness and welfare.

c. Is sensitive to cultural and social diversity among families and recognizes that all parents, custodial and noncustodial, are vested with certain rights and responsibilities for the welfare of their children by virtue of their role and according to law.

B.2. Parents and Confidentiality

The professional school counselor:

a. Informs parents of the counselor's role with emphasis on the confidential nature of the counseling relationship between the counselor and counselee.

b. Provides parents with accurate, comprehensive, and relevant information in an objective and caring manner, as is appropriate and consistent with ethical responsibilities to the counselee.

c. Makes reasonable efforts to honor the wishes of parents and guardians concerning information that he/she may share regarding the counselee.

C. Responsibilities to Colleagues and Professional Associates

C.1. Professional Relationships

The professional school counselor:

a. Establishes and maintains professional relationships with faculty, staff, and administration to facilitate the provision of optimal counseling services. The relationship is based on the counselor's definition and description of the parameter and levels of his or her professional roles.

b. Treats colleagues with professional respect, courtesy, and fairness. The qualifications, views, and findings of colleagues are represented to accurately reflect the image of competent professionals.

c. aware of and optimally utilizes related professions and organizations to whom the counselee may be referred.

C.2. Sharing Information with Other Professionals

The professional school counselor:

a. Promotes awareness and adherence to appropriate guidelines regarding confidentiality; the distinction between public and private information; and staff consultation.

b. Provides professional personnel with accurate, objective, concise, and meaningful data necessary to adequately evaluate, counsel, and assist the counselee.

c. If a counselee is receiving services from another counselor or other mental health professional, the counselor, with client consent, will inform the other professional and develop clear agreements to avoid confusion and conflict for the counselee.

D. Responsibilities to the School and Community

D.1. Responsibilities to the School

The professional school counselor:

a. Supports and protects the educational program against any infringement not in the best interest of counselees.

b. Informs appropriate officials of conditions that may be potentially disruptive or damaging to the school's mission, personnel, and property while honoring the confidentiality between the counselee and counselor.

c. Delineates and promotes the counselor's role and function in meeting the needs of those served. The counselor will notify appropriate officials of conditions which may limit or curtail her or his effectiveness in providing programs and services.

d. Accepts employment only for positions for which he/she is qualified by education, training, supervised experience, state and national professional credentials, and appropriate professional experience. Counselors recommend that administrators hire only qualified and competent individuals for professional counseling positions.

e. Assists in developing: (1) curricular and environmental conditions appropriate for the school and community; (2) educational procedures and programs to meet the counselee's developmental needs; and (3) a systematic evaluation process for comprehensive school counseling programs, services, and personnel. The counselor is guided by the findings of the evaluation data in planning programs and services.

D.2. Responsibility to the Community

The professional school counselor:

collaborates with agencies, organizations, and individuals in the school and community in the best interest of counselees and without regard to personal reward or remuneration.

E. Responsibilities to Self

E.1. Professional Competence

The professional school counselor:

a. Functions within the boundaries of individual professional competence and accepts responsibility for the consequences of his or her actions.

b. Monitors personal functioning and effectiveness and does not participate in any activity which may lead to inadequate professional services or harm to a client.

c. Strives through personal initiative to maintain professional competence and to keep abreast of professional information. Professional and personal growth are ongoing throughout the counselor's career.

E.2. Multicultural Skills

The professional school counselor:

understands the diverse cultural backgrounds of the counselees with whom he/she works. This includes, but is not limited to, learning how the school counselor's own cultural/ethnic/racial identity impacts her or his values and beliefs about the counseling process.

F. Responsibilities to the Profession

F.1. Professionalism

The professional school counselor:

a. Accepts the policies and processes for handling ethical violations as a result of maintaining membership in the American School Counselor Association.

b. Conducts herself/himself in such a manner as to advance individual ethical practice and the profession.

c. Conducts appropriate research and reports findings in a manner consistent with acceptable educational and psychological research practices. When using client data for research or for statistical or program planning purposes, the counselor ensures protection of the individual counselee's identity.

d. Adheres to ethical standards of the profession, other official policy statements pertaining to counseling, and relevant statutes established by federal, state, and local governments.

e.   Clearly distinguishes between statements and actions made as a private individual and those made as a representative of the school counseling profession.

f.   Does not use his or her professional position to recruit or gain clients, consultees for her or his private practice, seek and receive unjustified personal gains, unfair advantage, sexual favors, or unearned goods or services.

F.2. Contribution to the Profession

The professional school counselor:

a.   Actively participates in local, state, and national associations which foster the development and improvement of school counseling.

b.   Contributes to the development of the profession through sharing skills, ideas, and expertise with colleagues.

G. Maintenance of Standards

Ethical behavior among professional school counselors, Association members and nonmembers, is expected at all times. When there exists serious doubt as to the ethical behavior of colleagues, or if counselors are forced to work in situations or abide by policies which do not reflect the standards as outlined in these Ethical Standards for School Counselors, the counselor is obligated to take appropriate action to rectify the condition. The following procedure may serve as a guide:

1.   The counselor should consult confidentially with a professional colleague to discuss the nature of a complaint to see if she/he views the situation as an ethical violation.

2.   When feasible, the counselor should directly approach the colleague whose behavior is in question to discuss the complaint and seek resolution.

3.   If resolution is not forthcoming at the personal level, the counselor shall utilize the channels established within the school, school district, the state SCA, and ASCA Ethics Committee.

4. If the matter still remains unresolved, referral for review and appropriate
    action should be made to the Ethics Committees in the following sequence:
    - state school counselor association
    - American School Counselor Association

5. The ASCA Ethics Committee is responsible for educating--and consulting
    with – the membership regarding ethical standards. The Committee
    periodically reviews an recommends changes in code. The Committee will
    also receive and process questions to clarify the application of such
    standards. Questions must be submitted in writing to the ASCA Ethics
    Chair. Finally, the Committee will handle complaints of alleged violations
    of our ethical standards. Therefore, at the national level, complaints should
    be submitted in writing to the ASCA Ethics Committee, c/o the Executive
    Director, American School Counselor Association, 801 North Fairfax, Suite
    310, Alexandria, VA 22314.

H. Resources

School counselors are responsible for being aware of, and acting in accord with,
standards and positions of the counseling profession as represented in official
documents such as those listed below:

American Counseling Association. (1995). Code of ethics and standards of
practice. Alexandria, VA. (5999 Stevenson Ave., Alexandria, VA 22034) 1 800
347 6647 www.counseling.org.

American School Counselor Association. (1997). The national standards for
school counseling programs. Alexandria, VA. (801 North Fairfax Street, Suite
310, Alexandria, VA 22314) 1 800 306 4722 www.schoolcounselor.org.

American School Counselor Association. (1998). Position Statements.
Alexandria, VA.

American School Counselor Association. (1998). Professional liability
insurance program. (Brochure). Alexandria, VA.

Arrendondo, Toperek, Brown, Jones, Locke, Sanchez, and Stadler. (1996).
Multicultural counseling competencies and standards. Journal of Multicultural
Counseling and Development . Vol. 24, No. 1. See American Counseling
Association.

Arthur, G.L. and Swanson, C.D. (1993). Confidentiality and privileged communication. (1993). See American Counseling Association.

Association for Specialists in Group Work. (1989). Ethical Guidelines for group counselors. (1989). Alexandria, VA. See American Counseling Association.

Corey, G., Corey, M.S. and Callanan. (1998). Issues and Ethics in the Helping Professions. Pacific Grove, CA: Brooks/Cole. (Brooks/Cole, 511 Forest Lodge Rd., Pacific Grove, CA 93950) www.thomson.com.

Crawford, R. (1994). Avoiding counselor malpractice. Alexandria, VA. See American Counseling Association.

Forrester-Miller, H. and Davis, T.E. (1996). A practitioner's guide to ethical decision making. Alexandria, VA. See American Counseling Association.

Herlihy, B. and Corey, G. (1996). ACA ethical standards casebook. Fifth ed. Alexandria, VA. See American Counseling Association.

Herlihy, B. and Corey, G. (1992). Dual relationships in counseling. Alexandria, VA. See American Counseling Association.

Huey, W.C. and Remley, T.P. (1988). Ethical and legal issues in school counseling. Alexandria, VA. See American School Counselor Association.

Joint Committee on Testing Practices. (1988). Code of fair testing practices in education. Washington, DC: American Psychological Association. (1200 17th Street, NW, Washington, DC 20036) 202 336 5500

Mitchell, R.W. (1991). Documentation in counseling records. Alexandria, VA. See American Counseling Association.

National Board for Certified Counselors. (1998). National board for certified counselors: code of ethics. Greensboro, NC. (3 Terrace Way, Suite D, Greensboro, NC 27403-3660) 336 547 0607 www.nbcc.org.

National Board for Certified Counselors. (1997). Standards for the ethical practice of webcounseling. Greensboro, NC.

National Peer Helpers Association. (1989). Code of ethics for peer helping professionals. Greenville, NC. PO Box 2684, Greenville, NC 27836. 919 522 3959. nphaorg@aol.com.

Salo, M. and Schumate, S. (1993). Counseling minor clients. Alexandria, VA. See American School Counselor Association.

Stevens-Smith, P. and Hughes, M. (1993). Legal issues in marriage and family counseling. Alexandria, VA. See American School Counselor Association.

Wheeler, N. and Bertram, B. (1994). Legal aspects of counseling: avoiding lawsuits and legal problems. (Videotape). Alexandria, VA. See American School Counselor Association.

Ethical Standards for School Counselors was adopted by the ASCA Delegate Assembly, March 19, 1984. The first revision was approved by the ASCA Delegate Assembly, March 27, 1992. The second revision was approved by the ASCA Governing Board on March 30, 1998 and adopted on June 25, 1998.

Job Bank | Privacy Policy | Ethics | Search | Site Map
801 N. Fairfax St., Suite 310, Alexandria, VA 22314, (703) 683-ASCA

Appendix A-4
American Association for Marriage and Family Therapy

AAMFT Code of Ethics
Effective July 1, 2001

Preamble

The Board of Directors of the American Association for Marriage and Family Therapy (AAMFT) hereby promulgates, pursuant to Article 2, Section 2.013 of the Association's Bylaws, the Revised AAMFT Code of Ethics, effective July 1, 2001.

The AAMFT strives to honor the public trust in marriage and family therapists by setting standards for ethical practice as described in this Code. The ethical standards define professional expectations and are enforced by the AAMFT Ethics Committee. The absence of an explicit reference to a specific behavior or situation in the Code does not mean that the behavior is ethical or unethical. The standards are not exhaustive. Marriage and family therapists who are uncertain about the ethics of a particular course of action are encouraged to seek counsel from consultants, attorneys, supervisors, colleagues, or other appropriate authorities.

Both law and ethics govern the practice of marriage and family therapy. When making decisions regarding professional behavior, marriage and family therapists must consider the AAMFT Code of Ethics and applicable laws and regulations. If the AAMFT Code of Ethics prescribes a standard higher than that required by law, marriage and family therapists must meet the higher standard of the AAMFT Code of Ethics. Marriage and family therapists comply with the mandates of law, but make known their commitment to the AAMFT Code of Ethics and take steps to resolve the conflict in a responsible manner. The AAMFT supports legal mandates for reporting of alleged unethical conduct.

The AAMFT Code of Ethics is binding on Members of AAMFT in all membership categories, AAMFT-Approved Supervisors, and applicants for membership and the Approved Supervisor designation (hereafter, AAMFT Member). AAMFT members have an obligation to be familiar with the AAMFT Code of Ethics and its application to their professional services. Lack of awareness or misunderstanding of an ethical standard is not a defense to a charge of unethical conduct.

The process for filing, investigating, and resolving complaints of unethical conduct is described in the current Procedures for Handling Ethical Matters of the AAMFT Ethics Committee. Persons accused are considered innocent by the Ethics Committee until proven guilty, except as otherwise provided, and are entitled to due process. If an AAMFT Member resigns in anticipation of, or during the course of, an ethics investigation, the Ethics Committee will complete its investigation. Any publication of action taken by the Association will include the fact that the Member attempted to resign during the investigation.

Contents

Principle I
Responsibility to Clients

Marriage and family therapists advance the welfare of families and individuals They respect the rights of those persons seeking their assistance, and make reasonable efforts to ensure that their services are used appropriately.

1.1 Marriage and family therapists provide professional assistance to persons without discrimination on the basis of race, age, ethnicity, socioeconomic status, disability, gender, health status, religion, national origin, or sexual orientation.

1.2 Marriage and family therapists obtain appropriate informed consent to therapy or related procedures as early as feasible in the therapeutic relationship, and use language that is reasonably understandable to clients. The content of informed consent may vary depending upon the client and treatment plan; however, informed consent generally necessitates that the client: (a) has the capacity to consent; (b) has been adequately informed of significant information concerning treatment processes and procedures; (c) has been adequately informed of potential risks and benefits of treatments for which generally recognized standards do not yet exist; (d) has freely and without undue influence expressed consent; and (e) has provided consent that is appropriately documented. When persons, due to age or mental status, are legally incapable of giving informed consent, marriage and family therapists obtain informed permission from a legally authorized person, if such substitute consent is legally permissible.

1.3 Marriage and family therapists are aware of their influential positions with respect to clients, and they avoid exploiting the trust and dependency of such persons. Therapists, therefore, make every effort to avoid conditions and multiple relationships with clients that could impair professional judgment or increase the risk of exploitation. Such relationships include, but are not limited to, business or close personal relationships with a client or the client's immediate family. When the risk of impairment or exploitation exists due to conditions or multiple roles, therapists take appropriate precautions.

1.4 Sexual intimacy with clients is prohibited.

1.5 Sexual intimacy with former clients is likely to be harmful and is therefore prohibited for two years following the termination of therapy or last professional contact. In an effort to avoid exploiting the trust and dependency of clients, marriage and family therapists should not engage in sexual intimacy with former clients after the two years following termination or last professional contact. Should therapists engage in sexual intimacy with former clients following two years after termination or last professional contact, the burden shifts to the therapist to demonstrate that there has been no exploitation or injury to the former client or to the client's immediate family.

1.6 Marriage and family therapists comply with applicable laws regarding the reporting of alleged unethical conduct.

1.7 Marriage and family therapists do not use their professional relationships with clients to further their own interests.

1.8 Marriage and family therapists respect the rights of clients to make decisions and help them to understand the consequences of these decisions. Therapists clearly advise the clients that they have the responsibility to make decisions regarding relationships such as cohabitation, marriage, divorce, separation, reconciliation, custody, and visitation.

1.9 Marriage and family therapists continue therapeutic relationships only so long as it is reasonably clear that clients are benefiting from the relationship.

1.10 Marriage and family therapists assist persons in obtaining other therapeutic services if the therapist is unable or unwilling, for appropriate reasons, to provide professional help.

1.11 Marriage and family therapists do not abandon or neglect clients in treatment without making reasonable arrangements for the continuation of such treatment.

1.12 Marriage and family therapists obtain written informed consent from clients before videotaping, audio recording, or permitting third-party observation.

1.13 Marriage and family therapists, upon agreeing to provide services to a person or entity at the request of a third party, clarify, to the extent feasible and at the outset of the service, the nature of the relationship with each party and the limits of confidentiality.

Principle II
Confidentiality

Marriage and family therapists have unique confidentiality concerns because the client in a therapeutic relationship may be more than one person Therapists respect and guard the confidences of each individual client

2.1 Marriage and family therapists disclose to clients and other interested parties, as early as feasible in their professional contacts, the nature of confidentiality and possible limitations of the clients' right to confidentiality. Therapists review with clients the circumstances where confidential information may be requested and where disclosure of confidential information may be legally required. Circumstances may necessitate repeated disclosures.

2.2 Marriage and family therapists do not disclose client confidences except by written authorization or waiver, or where mandated or permitted by law. Verbal authorization will not be sufficient except in emergency situations, unless prohibited by law. When providing couple, family or group treatment, the therapist does not disclose information outside the treatment context without a written authorization from each individual competent to execute a waiver. In the context of couple, family or group treatment, the therapist may not reveal any individual's confidences to others in the client unit without the prior written permission of that individual.

2.3 Marriage and family therapists use client and/or clinical materials in teaching, writing, consulting, research, and public presentations only if a written waiver has been obtained in accordance with Subprinciple 2.2, or when appropriate steps have been taken to protect client identity and confidentiality.

2.4 Marriage and family therapists store, safeguard, and dispose of client records in ways that maintain confidentiality and in accord with applicable laws and professional standards.

2.5 Subsequent to the therapist moving from the area, closing the practice, or upon the death of the therapist, a marriage and family therapist arranges for the storage, transfer, or disposal of client records in ways that maintain confidentiality and safeguard the welfare of clients.

2.6 Marriage and family therapists, when consulting with colleagues or referral sources, do not share confidential information that could reasonably lead to the identification of a client, research participant, supervisee, or other person with whom they have a confidential relationship unless they have obtained the prior written consent of the client, research participant, supervisee, or other person with whom they have a confidential relationship. Information may be shared only to the extent necessary to achieve the purposes of the consultation.

Principle III
Professional Competence and Integrity

Marriage and family therapists maintain high standards of professional competence and integrity

3.1 Marriage and family therapists pursue knowledge of new developments and maintain competence in marriage and family therapy through education, training, or supervised experience.

3.2 Marriage and family therapists maintain adequate knowledge of and adhere to applicable laws, ethics, and professional standards.

3.3 Marriage and family therapists seek appropriate professional assistance for their personal problems or conflicts that may impair work performance or clinical judgment.

3.4 Marriage and family therapists do not provide services that create a conflict of interest that may impair work performance or clinical judgment.

3.5 Marriage and family therapists, as presenters, teachers, supervisors, consultants and researchers, are dedicated to high standards of scholarship, present accurate information, and disclose potential conflicts of interest.

3.6 Marriage and family therapists maintain accurate and adequate clinical and financial records.

3.7 While developing new skills in specialty areas, marriage and family therapists take steps to ensure the competence of their work and to protect clients from possible harm. Marriage and family therapists practice in specialty areas new to them only after appropriate education, training, or supervised experience.

3.8 Marriage and family therapists do not engage in sexual or other forms of harassment of clients, students, trainees, supervisees, employees, colleagues, or research subjects.

3.9 Marriage and family therapists do not engage in the exploitation of clients, students, trainees, supervisees, employees, colleagues, or research subjects.

3.10 Marriage and family therapists do not give to or receive from clients (a) gifts of substantial value or (b) gifts that impair the integrity or efficacy of the therapeutic relationship.

3.11 Marriage and family therapists do not diagnose, treat, or advise on problems outside the recognized boundaries of their competencies.

3.12 Marriage and family therapists make efforts to prevent the distortion or misuse of their clinical and research findings.

3.13 Marriage and family therapists, because of their ability to influence and alter the lives of others, exercise special care when making public their professional recommendations and opinions through testimony or other public statements.

3.14 To avoid a conflict of interests, marriage and family therapists who treat minors or adults involved in custody or visitation actions may not also perform forensic evaluations for custody, residence, or visitation of the minor. The marriage and family therapist who treats the minor may provide the court or mental health professional performing the evaluation with information about the minor from the marriage and family therapist's perspective as a treating marriage and family therapist, so long as the marriage and family therapist does not violate confidentiality.

3.15 Marriage and family therapists are in violation of this Code and subject to termination of membership or other appropriate action if they: (a) are convicted of any felony; (b) are convicted of a misdemeanor related to their qualifications or functions; (c) engage in conduct which could lead to conviction of a felony, or a misdemeanor related to their qualifications or functions; (d) are expelled from or disciplined by other professional organizations; (e) have their licenses or certificates suspended or revoked or are otherwise disciplined by regulatory bodies; (f) continue to practice marriage and family therapy while no longer competent to do so because they are impaired by physical or mental causes or the abuse of alcohol or other substances; or (g) fail to cooperate with the Association at any point from the inception of an ethical complaint through the completion of all proceedings regarding that complaint.

Principle IV
Responsibility to Students and Supervisees

Marriage and family therapists do not exploit the trust and dependency of students and supervisees

4.1 Marriage and family therapists are aware of their influential positions with respect to students and supervisees, and they avoid exploiting the trust and dependency of such persons. Therapists, therefore, make every effort to avoid conditions and multiple relationships that could impair professional objectivity or increase the risk of exploitation. When the risk of impairment or exploitation exists due to conditions or multiple roles, therapists take appropriate precautions.

4.2 Marriage and family therapists do not provide therapy to current students or supervisees.

4.3 Marriage and family therapists do not engage in sexual intimacy with students or supervisees during the evaluative or training relationship between the therapist and student or supervisee. Should a supervisor engage in sexual activity with a former supervisee, the burden of proof shifts to the supervisor to demonstrate that there has been no exploitation or injury to the supervisee.

4.4 Marriage and family therapists do not permit students or supervisees to perform or to hold themselves out as competent to perform professional services beyond their training, level of experience, and competence.

4.5 Marriage and family therapists take reasonable measures to ensure that services provided by supervisees are professional.

4.6 Marriage and family therapists avoid accepting as supervisees or students those individuals with whom a prior or existing relationship could compromise the therapist's objectivity. When such situations cannot be avoided, therapists take appropriate precautions to maintain objectivity. Examples of such relationships include, but are not limited to, those individuals with whom the therapist has a current or prior sexual, close personal, immediate familial, or therapeutic relationship.

4.7 Marriage and family therapists do not disclose supervisee confidences except by written authorization or waiver, or when mandated or permitted by law. In educational or training settings where there are multiple supervisors, disclosures are permitted only to other professional colleagues, administrators, or employers who share responsibility for training of the supervisee. Verbal authorization will not be sufficient except in emergency situations, unless prohibited by law.

Principle V
Responsibility to Research Participants

Investigators respect the dignity and protect the welfare of research participants, and are aware of applicable laws and regulations and professional standards governing the conduct of research

5. 1 Investigators are responsible for making careful examinations of ethical acceptability in planning studies. To the extent that services to research participants may be compromised by participation in research, investigators seek the ethical advice of qualified professionals not directly involved in the

investigation and observe safeguards to protect the rights of research participants.

5. 2 Investigators requesting participant involvement in research inform participants of the aspects of the research that might reasonably be expected to influence willingness to participate. Investigators are especially sensitive to the possibility of diminished consent when participants are also receiving clinical services, or have impairments which limit understanding and/or communication, or when participants are children.

5.3 Investigators respect each participant's freedom to decline participation in or to withdraw from a research study at any time. This obligation requires special thought and consideration when investigators or other members of the research team are in positions of authority or influence over participants. Marriage and family therapists, therefore, make every effort to avoid multiple relationships with research participants that could impair professional judgment or increase the risk of exploitation.

5.4 Information obtained about a research participant during the course of an investigation is confidential unless there is a waiver previously obtained in writing. When the possibility exists that others, including family members, may obtain access to such information, this possibility, together with the plan for protecting confidentiality, is explained as part of the procedure for obtaining informed consent.

Principle VI
Responsibility to the Profession

Marriage and family therapists respect the rights and responsibilities of professional colleagues and participate in activities that advance the goals of the profession.

6.1 Marriage and family therapists remain accountable to the standards of the profession when acting as members or employees of organizations. If the mandates of an organization with which a marriage and family therapist is affiliated, through employment, contract or otherwise, conflict with the AAMFT Code of Ethics, marriage and family therapists make known to the organization their commitment to the AAMFT Code of Ethics and attempt to resolve the conflict in a way that allows the fullest adherence to the Code of Ethics.

6.2 Marriage and family therapists assign publication credit to those who have contributed to a publication in proportion to their contributions and in accordance with customary professional publication practices.

6.3 Marriage and family therapists do not accept or require authorship credit for a publication based on research from a student's program, unless the therapist made a substantial contribution beyond being a faculty advisor or research committee member. Coauthorship on a student thesis, dissertation, or project should be determined in accordance with principles of fairness and justice.

6.4 Marriage and family therapists who are the authors of books or other materials that are published or distributed do not plagiarize or fail to cite persons to whom credit for original ideas or work is due.

6.5 Marriage and family therapists who are the authors of books or other materials published or distributed by an organization take reasonable precautions to ensure that the organization promotes and advertises the materials accurately and factually.

6.6 Marriage and family therapists participate in activities that contribute to a better community and society, including devoting a portion of their professional activity to services for which there is little or no financial return.

6.7 Marriage and family therapists are concerned with developing laws and regulations pertaining to marriage and family therapy that serve the public interest, and with altering such laws and regulations that are not in the public interest.

6.8 Marriage and family therapists encourage public participation in the design and delivery of professional services and in the regulation of practitioners.

Principle VII
Financial Arrangements

Marriage and family therapists make financial arrangements with clients, third-party payors, and supervisees that are reasonably understandable and conform to accepted professional practices

7.1 Marriage and family therapists do not offer or accept kickbacks, rebates, bonuses, or other remuneration for referrals; fee-for-service arrangements are not prohibited.

7.2 Prior to entering into the therapeutic or supervisory relationship, marriage and family therapists clearly disclose and explain to clients and supervisees: (a) all financial arrangements and fees related to professional services, including charges for canceled or missed appointments; (b) the use of collection agencies or legal measures for nonpayment; and (c) the procedure for obtaining payment from the client, to the extent allowed by law, if payment is denied by the third-party payor. Once services have begun, therapists provide reasonable notice of any changes in fees or other charges.

7.3 Marriage and family therapists give reasonable notice to clients with unpaid balances of their intent to seek collection by agency or legal recourse. When such action is taken, therapists will not disclose clinical information.

7.4 Marriage and family therapists represent facts truthfully to clients, third-party payors, and supervisees regarding services rendered.

7.5 Marriage and family therapists ordinarily refrain from accepting goods and services from clients in return for services rendered. Bartering for professional services may be conducted only if: (a) the supervisee or client requests it, (b) the relationship is not exploitative, (c) the professional relationship is not distorted, and (d) a clear written contract is established.

7.6 Marriage and family therapists may not withhold records under their immediate control that are requested and needed for a client's treatment solely because payment has not been received for past services, except as otherwise provided by law.

Principle VIII
Advertising

Marriage and family therapists engage in appropriate informational activities, including those that enable the public, referral sources, or others to choose professional services on an informed basis.

8.1 Marriage and family therapists accurately represent their competencies, education, training, and experience relevant to their practice of marriage and family therapy.

8.2 Marriage and family therapists ensure that advertisements and publications in any media (such as directories, announcements, business cards, newspapers, radio, television, Internet, and facsimiles) convey information that is necessary for the public to make an appropriate selection of professional services. Information could include: (a) office information, such as name, address, telephone number, credit card acceptability, fees, languages spoken, and office hours; (b) qualifying clinical degree (see subprinciple 8.5); (c) other earned degrees (see subprinciple 8.5) and state or provincial licensures and/or certifications; (d) AAMFT clinical member status; and (e) description of practice.

8.3 Marriage and family therapists do not use names that could mislead the public concerning the identity, responsibility, source, and status of those practicing under that name, and do not hold themselves out as being partners or associates of a firm if they are not.

8.4 Marriage and family therapists do not use any professional identification (such as a business card, office sign, letterhead, Internet, or telephone or association directory listing) if it includes a statement or claim that is false, fraudulent, misleading, or deceptive.

8.5 In representing their educational qualifications, marriage and family therapists list and claim as evidence only those earned degrees: (a) from institutions accredited by regional accreditation sources recognized by the United States Department of Education, (b) from institutions recognized by states or provinces that license or certify marriage and family therapists, or (c) from equivalent foreign institutions.

8.6 Marriage and family therapists correct, wherever possible, false, misleading, or inaccurate information and representations made by others concerning the therapist's qualifications, services, or products.

8.7 Marriage and family therapists make certain that the qualifications of their employees or supervisees are represented in a manner that is not false, misleading, or deceptive.

8.8 Marriage and family therapists do not represent themselves as providing specialized services unless they have the appropriate education, training, or supervised experience.

This Code is published by:
American Association for Marriage and Family Therapy
112 South Alfred Street, Alexandria, VA 22314
Phone: (703) 838-9808 - Fax: (703) 838-9805
www.aamft.org

Appendix A-5
Code of Ethics
of the National Association of Social Workers

Approved by the 1996 NASW Delegate Assembly and revised by the 1999 NASW Delegate Assembly

Preamble

The primary mission of the social work profession is to enhance human well-being and help meet the basic human needs of all people, with particular attention to the needs and empowerment of people who are vulnerable, oppressed, and living in poverty. A historic and defining feature of social work is the profession's focus on individual well-being in a social context and the well-being of society. Fundamental to social work is attention to the environmental forces that create, contribute to, and address problems in living.

Social workers promote social justice and social change with and on behalf of clients. "Clients" is used inclusively to refer to individuals, families, groups, organizations, and communities. Social workers are sensitive to cultural and ethnic diversity and strive to end discrimination, oppression, poverty, and other forms of social injustice. These activities may be in the form of direct practice, community organizing, supervision, consultation, administration, advocacy, social and political action, policy development and implementation, education, and research and evaluation. Social workers seek to enhance the capacity of people to address their own needs. Social workers also seek to promote the responsiveness of organizations, communities, and other social institutions to individuals' needs and social problems.

The mission of the social work profession is rooted in a set of core values. These core values, embraced by social workers throughout the profession's history, are the foundation of social work's unique purpose and perspective:

- service
- social justice
- dignity and worth of the person
- importance of human relationships
- integrity
- competence.

This constellation of core values reflects what is unique to the social work profession. Core values, and the principles that flow from them, must be balanced within the context and complexity of the human experience.

Purpose of the NASW Code of Ethics

Professional ethics are at the core of social work. The profession has an obligation to articulate its basic values, ethical principles, and ethical standards. The sets forth these values, principles, and standards to guide social workers' conduct. The *Code* is relevant to all social workers and social work students, regardless of their professional functions, the settings in which they work, or the populations they serve.

The *NASW Code of Ethics* serves six purposes:

1. The *Code* identifies core values on which social work's mission is based.
2. The *Code* summarizes broad ethical principles that reflect the profession's core values and establishes a set of specific ethical standards that should be used to guide social work practice.
3. The *Code* is designed to help social workers identify relevant considerations when professional obligations conflict or ethical uncertainties arise.
4. The *Code* provides ethical standards to which the general public can hold the social work profession accountable.
5. The *Code* socializes practitioners new to the field to social work's mission, values, ethical principles, and ethical standards.
6. The *Code* articulates standards that the social work profession itself can use to assess whether social workers have engaged in unethical conduct. NASW has formal procedures to adjudicate ethics complaints filed against its members.* In subscribing to this *Code*, social workers are required to cooperate in its implementation, participate in NASW adjudication proceedings, and abide by any NASW disciplinary rulings or sanctions based on it.

*For information on NASW adjudication procedures, see NASW Procedures for the Adjudication of Grievances.

The *Code* offers a set of values, principles, and standards to guide decision making and conduct when ethical issues arise. It does not provide a set of rules that prescribe how social workers should act in all situations. Specific applications of the *Code* must take into account the context in which it is being considered and the possibility of conflicts among the *Code*'s values, principles, and standards. Ethical responsibilities flow from all human relationships, from the personal and familial to the social and professional.

Further, the *NASW Code of Ethics* does not specify which values, principles, and standards are most important and ought to outweigh others in instances when they conflict. Reasonable differences of opinion can and do exist among social workers with respect to the ways in which values, ethical principles, and ethical standards should be rank ordered when they conflict. Ethical decision making in a given situation must apply the informed judgment of the individual social worker and should also consider how the issues would be judged in a peer review process where the ethical standards of the profession would be applied.

Ethical decision making is a process. There are many instances in social work where simple answers are not available to resolve complex ethical issues. Social workers should take into consideration all the values, principles, and standards in this *Code* that are relevant to any situation in which ethical judgment is warranted. Social workers' decisions and actions should be consistent with the spirit as well as the letter of this *Code*.

In addition to this *Code*, there are many other sources of information about ethical thinking that may be useful. Social workers should consider ethical theory and principles generally, social work theory and research, laws, regulations, agency policies, and other relevant codes of ethics, recognizing that among codes of ethics social workers should consider the *NASW Code of Ethics* as their primary source. Social workers also should be aware of the impact on ethical decision making of their clients' and their own personal values and cultural and religious beliefs and practices. They should be aware of any conflicts between personal and professional values and deal with them responsibly. For additional guidance social workers should consult the relevant literature on professional ethics and ethical decision making and seek appropriate consultation when faced with ethical dilemmas. This may involve consultation with an agency-based or social work organization's ethics committee, a regulatory body, knowledgeable colleagues, supervisors, or legal counsel.

Instances may arise when social workers' ethical obligations conflict with agency policies or relevant laws or regulations. When such conflicts occur, social workers must make a responsible effort to resolve the conflict in a manner that is consistent with the values, principles, and standards expressed in this

Code. If a reasonable resolution of the conflict does not appear possible, social workers should seek proper consultation before making a decision.

The *NASW Code of Ethics* is to be used by NASW and by individuals, agencies, organizations, and bodies (such as licensing and regulatory boards, professional liability insurance providers, courts of law, agency boards of directors, government agencies, and other professional groups) that choose to adopt it or use it as a frame of reference. Violation of standards in this *Code* does not automatically imply legal liability or violation of the law. Such determination can only be made in the context of legal and judicial proceedings. Alleged violations of the *Code* would be subject to a peer review process. Such processes are generally separate from legal or administrative procedures and insulated from legal review or proceedings to allow the profession to counsel and discipline its own members.

A code of ethics cannot guarantee ethical behavior. Moreover, a code of ethics cannot resolve all ethical issues or disputes or capture the richness and complexity involved in striving to make responsible choices within a moral community. Rather, a code of ethics sets forth values, ethical principles, and ethical standards to which professionals aspire and by which their actions can be judged. Social workers' ethical behavior should result from their personal commitment to engage in ethical practice. The *NASW Code of Ethics* reflects the commitment of all social workers to uphold the profession's values and to act ethically. Principles and standards must be applied by individuals of good character who discern moral questions and, in good faith, seek to make reliable ethical judgments.

Ethical Principles

The following broad ethical principles are based on social work's core values of service, social justice, dignity and worth of the person, importance of human relationships, integrity, and competence. These principles set forth ideals to which all social workers should aspire.

Value: *Service*

Ethical Principle: *Social workers' primary goal is to help people in need and to address social problems*

Social workers elevate service to others above self-interest. Social workers draw on their knowledge, values, and skills to help people in need and to address social problems. Social workers are encouraged to volunteer some portion of their professional skills with no expectation of significant financial return (pro bono service).

Value: *Social Justice*

Ethical Principle: *Social workers challenge social injustice*

Social workers pursue social change, particularly with and on behalf of vulnerable and oppressed individuals and groups of people. Social workers' social change efforts are focused primarily on issues of poverty, unemployment, discrimination, and other forms of social injustice. These activities seek to promote sensitivity to and knowledge about oppression and cultural and ethnic diversity. Social workers strive to ensure access to needed information, services, and resources; equality of opportunity; and meaningful participation in decision making for all people.

Value: *Dignity and Worth of the Person*

Ethical Principle: *Social workers respect the inherent dignity and worth of the person*

Social workers treat each person in a caring and respectful fashion, mindful of individual differences and cultural and ethnic diversity. Social workers promote clients' socially responsible self-determination. Social workers seek to enhance clients' capacity and opportunity to change and to address their own needs. Social workers are cognizant of their dual responsibility to clients and to the broader society. They seek to resolve conflicts between clients' interests and the broader society's interests in a socially responsible manner consistent with the values, ethical principles, and ethical standards of the profession.

Value: *Importance of Human Relationships*

Ethical Principle: *Social workers recognize the central importance of human relationships*

Social workers understand that relationships between and among people are an important vehicle for change. Social workers engage people as partners in the helping process. Social workers seek to strengthen relationships among people in a purposeful effort to promote, restore, maintain, and enhance the well-being of individuals, families, social groups, organizations, and communities.

Value: *Integrity*

Ethical Principle: *Social workers behave in a trustworthy manner*

Social workers are continually aware of the profession's mission, values, ethical principles, and ethical standards and practice in a manner consistent with them. Social workers act honestly and responsibly and promote ethical practices on the part of the organizations with which they are affiliated.

Value: *Competence*

Ethical Principle: *Social workers practice within their areas of competence and develop and enhance their professional expertise*

Social workers continually strive to increase their professional knowledge and skills and to apply them in practice. Social workers should aspire to contribute to the knowledge base of the profession.

Ethical Standards

The following ethical standards are relevant to the professional activities of all social workers. These standards concern (1) social workers' ethical responsibilities to clients, (2) social workers' ethical responsibilities to colleagues, (3) social workers' ethical responsibilities in practice settings, (4) social workers' ethical responsibilities as professionals, (5) social workers' ethical responsibilities to the social work profession, and (6) social workers' ethical responsibilities to the broader society.

Some of the standards that follow are enforceable guidelines for professional conduct, and some are aspirational. The extent to which each standard is enforceable is a matter of professional judgment to be exercised by those responsible for reviewing alleged violations of ethical standards.

1. Social Workers' Ethical Responsibilities to Clients

1.01 Commitment to Clients

Social workers' primary responsibility is to promote the well-being of clients. In general, clients' interests are primary. However, social workers' responsibility to the larger society or specific legal obligations may on limited occasions supersede the loyalty owed clients, and clients should be so advised. (Examples include when a social worker is required by law to report that a client has abused a child or has threatened to harm self or others.)

1.02 Self-Determination

Social workers respect and promote the right of clients to self-determination and assist clients in their efforts to identify and clarify their goals. Social workers may limit clients' right to self-determination when, in the social workers' professional judgment, clients' actions or potential actions pose a serious, foreseeable, and imminent risk to themselves or others.

1.03 Informed Consent

(a) Social workers should provide services to clients only in the context of a professional relationship based, when appropriate, on valid informed consent. Social workers should use clear and understandable language to inform clients of the purpose of the services, risks related to the services, limits to services because of the requirements of a third-party payer, relevant costs, reasonable alternatives, clients' right to refuse or withdraw consent, and the time frame covered by the consent. Social workers should provide clients with an opportunity to ask questions.

(b) In instances when clients are not literate or have difficulty understanding the primary language used in the practice setting, social workers should take steps to ensure clients' comprehension. This may include providing clients with a detailed verbal explanation or arranging for a qualified interpreter or translator whenever possible.

(c) In instances when clients lack the capacity to provide informed consent, social workers should protect clients' interests by seeking permission from an appropriate third party, informing clients consistent with the clients' level of understanding. In such instances social workers should seek to ensure that the third party acts in a manner consistent with clients' wishes and interests. Social workers should take reasonable steps to enhance such clients' ability to give informed consent.

(d) In instances when clients are receiving services involuntarily, social workers should provide information about the nature and extent of services and about the extent of clients' right to refuse service.

(e) Social workers who provide services via electronic media (such as computer, telephone, radio, and television) should inform recipients of the limitations and risks associated with such services.

(f) Social workers should obtain clients' informed consent before audiotaping or videotaping clients or permitting observation of services to clients by a third party.

1.04 Competence

(a) Social workers should provide services and represent themselves as competent only within the boundaries of their education, training, license, certification, consultation received, supervised experience, or other relevant professional experience.

(b) Social workers should provide services in substantive areas or use intervention techniques or approaches that are new to them only after engaging in appropriate study, training, consultation, and supervision from people who are competent in those interventions or techniques.

(c) When generally recognized standards do not exist with respect to an emerging area of practice, social workers should exercise careful judgment and take responsible steps (including appropriate education, research, training, consultation, and supervision) to ensure the competence of their work and to protect clients from harm.

1.05 Cultural Competence and Social Diversity

(a) Social workers should understand culture and its function in human behavior and society, recognizing the strengths that exist in all cultures.

(b) Social workers should have a knowledge base of their clients' cultures and be able to demonstrate competence in the provision of services that are sensitive to clients' cultures and to differences among people and cultural groups.
(c) Social workers should obtain education about and seek to understand the nature of social diversity and oppression with respect to race, ethnicity, national origin, color, sex, sexual orientation, age, marital status, political belief, religion, and mental or physical disability.

1.06 Conflicts of Interest

(a) Social workers should be alert to and avoid conflicts of interest that interfere with the exercise of professional discretion and impartial judgment. Social workers should inform clients when a real or potential conflict of interest arises and take reasonable steps to resolve the issue in a manner that makes the clients' interests primary and protects clients' interests to the greatest extent possible. In some cases, protecting clients' interests may require termination of the professional relationship with proper referral of the client.

(b) Social workers should not take unfair advantage of any professional relationship or exploit others to further their personal, religious, political, or business interests.

(c) Social workers should not engage in dual or multiple relationships with clients or former clients in which there is a risk of exploitation or potential harm to the client. In instances when dual or multiple relationships are unavoidable, social workers should take steps to protect clients and are responsible for setting clear, appropriate, and culturally sensitive boundaries. (Dual or multiple relationships occur when social workers relate to clients in more than one relationship, whether professional, social, or business. Dual or multiple relationships can occur simultaneously or consecutively.)

(d) When social workers provide services to two or more people who have a relationship with each other (for example, couples, family members), social workers should clarify with all parties which individuals will be considered clients and the nature of social workers' professional obligations to the various individuals who are receiving services. Social workers who anticipate a conflict of interest among the individuals receiving services or who anticipate having to perform in potentially conflicting roles (for example, when a social worker is asked to testify in a child custody dispute or divorce proceedings involving clients) should clarify their role with the parties involved and take appropriate action to minimize any conflict of interest.

1.07 Privacy and Confidentiality

(a) Social workers should respect clients' right to privacy. Social workers should not solicit private information from clients unless it is essential to providing services or conducting social work evaluation or research. Once private information is shared, standards of confidentiality apply.

(b) Social workers may disclose confidential information when appropriate with valid consent from a client or a person legally authorized to consent on behalf of a client.

(c) Social workers should protect the confidentiality of all information obtained in the course of professional service, except for compelling professional reasons. The general expectation that social workers will keep information confidential does not apply when disclosure is necessary to prevent serious, foreseeable, and imminent harm to a client or other identifiable person. In all instances, social workers should disclose the least amount of confidential information necessary to achieve the desired purpose; only information that is directly relevant to the purpose for which the disclosure is made should be revealed.

(d) Social workers should inform clients, to the extent possible, about the disclosure of confidential information and the potential consequences, when feasible before the disclosure is made. This applies whether social workers disclose confidential information on the basis of a legal requirement or client consent.

(e) Social workers should discuss with clients and other interested parties the nature of confidentiality and limitations of clients' right to confidentiality. Social workers should review with clients circumstances where confidential information may be requested and where disclosure of confidential information may be legally required. This discussion should occur as soon as possible in the social worker-client relationship and as needed throughout the course of the relationship.

(f) When social workers provide counseling services to families, couples, or groups, social workers should seek agreement among the parties involved concerning each individual's right to confidentiality and obligation to preserve the confidentiality of information shared by others. Social workers should inform participants in family, couples, or group counseling that social workers cannot guarantee that all participants will honor such agreements.

(g) Social workers should inform clients involved in family, couples, marital, or group counseling of the social worker's, employer's, and agency's policy concerning the social worker's disclosure of confidential information among the parties involved in the counseling.

(h) Social workers should not disclose confidential information to third-party payers unless clients have authorized such disclosure.

(i) Social workers should not discuss confidential information in any setting unless privacy can be ensured. Social workers should not discuss confidential information in public or semipublic areas such as hallways, waiting rooms, elevators, and restaurants.

(j) Social workers should protect the confidentiality of clients during legal proceedings to the extent permitted by law. When a court of law or other legally authorized body orders social workers to disclose confidential or privileged information without a client's consent and such disclosure could cause harm to the client, social workers should request that the court withdraw the order or limit the order as narrowly as possible or maintain the records under seal, unavailable for public inspection.

(k) Social workers should protect the confidentiality of clients when responding to requests from members of the media.

(l) Social workers should protect the confidentiality of clients' written and electronic records and other sensitive information. Social workers should take reasonable steps to ensure that clients' records are stored in a secure location and that clients' records are not available to others who are not authorized to have access.

(m) Social workers should take precautions to ensure and maintain the confidentiality of information transmitted to other parties through the use of computers, electronic mail, facsimile machines, telephones and telephone answering machines, and other electronic or computer technology. Disclosure of identifying information should be avoided whenever possible.

(n) Social workers should transfer or dispose of clients' records in a manner that protects clients' confidentiality and is consistent with state statutes governing records and social work licensure.

(o) Social workers should take reasonable precautions to protect client confidentiality in the event of the social worker's termination of practice, incapacitation, or death.

(p) Social workers should not disclose identifying information when discussing clients for teaching or training purposes unless the client has consented to disclosure of confidential information.

(q) Social workers should not disclose identifying information when discussing clients with consultants unless the client has consented to disclosure of confidential information or there is a compelling need for such disclosure.

(r) Social workers should protect the confidentiality of deceased clients consistent with the preceding standards.

1.08 Access to Records

(a) Social workers should provide clients with reasonable access to records concerning the clients. Social workers who are concerned that clients' access to their records could cause serious misunderstanding or harm to the client should provide assistance in interpreting the records and consultation with the client regarding the records. Social workers should limit clients' access to their records, or portions of their records, only in exceptional circumstances when there is compelling evidence that such access would cause serious harm to the client. Both clients' requests and the rationale for withholding some or all of the record should be documented in clients' files.

(b) When providing clients with access to their records, social workers should take steps to protect the confidentiality of other individuals identified or discussed in such records.

1.09 Sexual Relationships

(a) Social workers should under no circumstances engage in sexual activities or sexual contact with current clients, whether such contact is consensual or forced.

(b) Social workers should not engage in sexual activities or sexual contact with clients' relatives or other individuals with whom clients maintain a close personal relationship when there is a risk of exploitation or potential harm to the client. Sexual activity or sexual contact with clients' relatives or other individuals with whom clients maintain a personal relationship has the potential to be harmful to the client and may make it difficult for the social worker and client to maintain appropriate professional boundaries. Social workers--not their clients, their clients' relatives, or other individuals with whom the client maintains a personal relationship--assume the full burden for setting clear, appropriate, and culturally sensitive boundaries.

(c) Social workers should not engage in sexual activities or sexual contact with former clients because of the potential for harm to the client. If social workers

•

engage in conduct contrary to this prohibition or claim that an exception to this prohibition is warranted because of extraordinary circumstances, it is social workers--not their clients--who assume the full burden of demonstrating that the former client has not been exploited, coerced, or manipulated, intentionally or unintentionally.

(d) Social workers should not provide clinical services to individuals with whom they have had a prior sexual relationship. Providing clinical services to a former sexual partner has the potential to be harmful to the individual and is likely to make it difficult for the social worker and individual to maintain appropriate professional boundaries.

1.10 Physical Contact

Social workers should not engage in physical contact with clients when there is a possibility of psychological harm to the client as a result of the contact (such as cradling or caressing clients). Social workers who engage in appropriate physical contact with clients are responsible for setting clear, appropriate, and culturally sensitive boundaries that govern such physical contact.

1.11 Sexual Harassment

Social workers should not sexually harass clients. Sexual harassment includes sexual advances, sexual solicitation, requests for sexual favors, and other verbal or physical conduct of a sexual nature.

1.12 Derogatory Language

Social workers should not use derogatory language in their written or verbal communications to or about clients. Social workers should use accurate and respectful language in all communications to and about clients.

1.13 Payment for Services

(a) When setting fees, social workers should ensure that the fees are fair, reasonable, and commensurate with the services performed. Consideration should be given to clients' ability to pay.

(b) Social workers should avoid accepting goods or services from clients as payment for professional services. Bartering arrangements, particularly involving services, create the potential for conflicts of interest, exploitation, and inappropriate boundaries in social workers' relationships with clients. Social workers should explore and may participate in bartering only in very limited circumstances when it can be demonstrated that such arrangements are an accepted practice among professionals in the local community, considered to be essential for the provision of services, negotiated without coercion, and entered into at the client's initiative and with the client's informed consent. Social workers who accept goods or services from clients as payment for professional services assume the full burden of demonstrating that this arrangement will not be detrimental to the client or the professional relationship.

(c) Social workers should not solicit a private fee or other remuneration for providing services to clients who are entitled to such available services through the social workers' employer or agency.

1.14 Clients Who Lack Decision-Making Capacity

When social workers act on behalf of clients who lack the capacity to make informed decisions, social workers should take reasonable steps to safeguard the interests and rights of those clients.

1.15 Interruption of Services

Social workers should make reasonable efforts to ensure continuity of services in the event that services are interrupted by factors such as unavailability, relocation, illness, disability, or death.

1.16 Termination of Services

(a) Social workers should terminate services to clients and professional relationships with them when such services and relationships are no longer required or no longer serve the clients' needs or interests.

(b) Social workers should take reasonable steps to avoid abandoning clients who are still in need of services. Social workers should withdraw services precipitously only under unusual circumstances, giving careful consideration to all factors in the situation and taking care to minimize possible adverse effects. Social workers should assist in making appropriate arrangements for continuation of services when necessary.

(c) Social workers in fee-for-service settings may terminate services to clients who are not paying an overdue balance if the financial contractual arrangements have been made clear to the client, if the client does not pose an imminent danger to self or others, and if the clinical and other consequences of the current nonpayment have been addressed and discussed with the client.

(d) Social workers should not terminate services to pursue a social, financial, or sexual relationship with a client.

(e) Social workers who anticipate the termination or interruption of services to clients should notify clients promptly and seek the transfer, referral, or continuation of services in relation to the clients' needs and preferences.

(f) Social workers who are leaving an employment setting should inform clients of appropriate options for the continuation of services and of the benefits and risks of the options.

2. Social Workers' Ethical Responsibilities to Colleagues

2.01 Respect

(a) Social workers should treat colleagues with respect and should represent accurately and fairly the qualifications, views, and obligations of colleagues.

(b) Social workers should avoid unwarranted negative criticism of colleagues in communications with clients or with other professionals. Unwarranted negative criticism may include demeaning comments that refer to colleagues' level of competence or to individuals' attributes such as race, ethnicity, national origin, color, sex, sexual orientation, age, marital status, political belief, religion, and mental or physical disability.

(c) Social workers should cooperate with social work colleagues and with colleagues of other professions when such cooperation serves the well-being of clients.

2.02 Confidentiality

Social workers should respect confidential information shared by colleagues in the course of their professional relationships and transactions. Social workers should ensure that such colleagues understand social workers' obligation to respect confidentiality and any exceptions related to it.

2.03 Interdisciplinary Collaboration

(a) Social workers who are members of an interdisciplinary team should participate in and contribute to decisions that affect the well-being of clients by drawing on the perspectives, values, and experiences of the social work profession. Professional and ethical obligations of the interdisciplinary team as a whole and of its individual members should be clearly established.

(b) Social workers for whom a team decision raises ethical concerns should attempt to resolve the disagreement through appropriate channels. If the disagreement cannot be resolved, social workers should pursue other avenues to address their concerns consistent with client well-being.

2.04 Disputes Involving Colleagues

(a) Social workers should not take advantage of a dispute between a colleague and an employer to obtain a position or otherwise advance the social workers' own interests.

(b) Social workers should not exploit clients in disputes with colleagues or engage clients in any inappropriate discussion of conflicts between social workers and their colleagues.

2.05 Consultation

(a) Social workers should seek the advice and counsel of colleagues whenever such consultation is in the best interests of clients.

(b) Social workers should keep themselves informed about colleagues' areas of expertise and competencies. Social workers should seek consultation only from colleagues who have demonstrated knowledge, expertise, and competence related to the subject of the consultation.

(c) When consulting with colleagues about clients, social workers should disclose the least amount of information necessary to achieve the purposes of the consultation.

2.06 Referral for Services

(a) Social workers should refer clients to other professionals when the other professionals' specialized knowledge or expertise is needed to serve clients fully or when social workers believe that they are not being effective or making reasonable progress with clients and that additional service is required.

(b) Social workers who refer clients to other professionals should take appropriate steps to facilitate an orderly transfer of responsibility. Social workers who refer clients to other professionals should disclose, with clients' consent, all pertinent information to the new service providers.

(c) Social workers are prohibited from giving or receiving payment for a referral when no professional service is provided by the referring social worker.

2.07 Sexual Relationships

(a) Social workers who function as supervisors or educators should not engage in sexual activities or contact with supervisees, students, trainees, or other colleagues over whom they exercise professional authority.

(b) Social workers should avoid engaging in sexual relationships with colleagues when there is potential for a conflict of interest. Social workers who become involved in, or anticipate becoming involved in, a sexual relationship with a colleague have a duty to transfer professional responsibilities, when necessary, to avoid a conflict of interest.

2.08 Sexual Harassment

Social workers should not sexually harass supervisees, students, trainees, or colleagues. Sexual harassment includes sexual advances, sexual solicitation, requests for sexual favors, and other verbal or physical conduct of a sexual nature.

2.09 Impairment of Colleagues

(a) Social workers who have direct knowledge of a social work colleague's impairment that is due to personal problems, psychosocial distress, substance abuse, or mental health difficulties and that interferes with practice effectiveness should consult with that colleague when feasible and assist the colleague in taking remedial action.

(b) Social workers who believe that a social work colleague's impairment interferes with practice effectiveness and that the colleague has not taken adequate steps to address the impairment should take action through appropriate channels established by employers, agencies, NASW, licensing and regulatory bodies, and other professional organizations.

2.10 Incompetence of Colleagues

(a) Social workers who have direct knowledge of a social work colleague's incompetence should consult with that colleague when feasible and assist the colleague in taking remedial action.

(b) Social workers who believe that a social work colleague is incompetent and has not taken adequate steps to address the incompetence should take action through appropriate channels established by employers, agencies, NASW, licensing and regulatory bodies, and other professional organizations.

2.11 Unethical Conduct of Colleagues

(a) Social workers should take adequate measures to discourage, prevent, expose, and correct the unethical conduct of colleagues.

(b) Social workers should be knowledgeable about established policies and procedures for handling concerns about colleagues' unethical behavior. Social workers should be familiar with national, state, and local procedures for handling ethics complaints. These include policies and procedures created by NASW, licensing and regulatory bodies, employers, agencies, and other professional organizations.

(c) Social workers who believe that a colleague has acted unethically should seek resolution by discussing their concerns with the colleague when feasible and when such discussion is likely to be productive.

(d) When necessary, social workers who believe that a colleague has acted unethically should take action through appropriate formal channels (such as contacting a state licensing board or regulatory body, an NASW committee on inquiry, or other professional ethics committees).

(e) Social workers should defend and assist colleagues who are unjustly charged with unethical conduct.

3. Social Workers' Ethical Responsibilities in Practice Settings

3.01 Supervision and Consultation

(a) Social workers who provide supervision or consultation should have the necessary knowledge and skill to supervise or consult appropriately and should do so only within their areas of knowledge and competence.

(b) Social workers who provide supervision or consultation are responsible for setting clear, appropriate, and culturally sensitive boundaries.

(c) Social workers should not engage in any dual or multiple relationships with supervisees in which there is a risk of exploitation of or potential harm to the supervisee.

(d) Social workers who provide supervision should evaluate supervisees' performance in a manner that is fair and respectful.

3.02 Education and Training

(a) Social workers who function as educators, field instructors for students, or trainers should provide instruction only within their areas of knowledge and competence and should provide instruction based on the most current information and knowledge available in the profession.

(b) Social workers who function as educators or field instructors for students should evaluate students' performance in a manner that is fair and respectful.

(c) Social workers who function as educators or field instructors for students should take reasonable steps to ensure that clients are routinely informed when services are being provided by students.

(d) Social workers who function as educators or field instructors for students should not engage in any dual or multiple relationships with students in which there is a risk of exploitation or potential harm to the student. Social work educators and field instructors are responsible for setting clear, appropriate, and culturally sensitive boundaries.

3.03 Performance Evaluation

Social workers who have responsibility for evaluating the performance of others should fulfill such responsibility in a fair and considerate manner and on the basis of clearly stated criteria.

3.04 Client Records

(a) Social workers should take reasonable steps to ensure that documentation in records is accurate and reflects the services provided.

(b) Social workers should include sufficient and timely documentation in records to facilitate the delivery of services and to ensure continuity of services provided to clients in the future.

(c) Social workers' documentation should protect clients' privacy to the extent that is possible and appropriate and should include only information that is directly relevant to the delivery of services.

(d) Social workers should store records following the termination of services to ensure reasonable future access. Records should be maintained for the number of years required by state statutes or relevant contracts.

3.05 Billing

Social workers should establish and maintain billing practices that accurately reflect the nature and extent of services provided and that identify who provided the service in the practice setting.

3.06 Client Transfer

(a) When an individual who is receiving services from another agency or colleague contacts a social worker for services, the social worker should carefully consider the client's needs before agreeing to provide services. To minimize possible confusion and conflict, social workers should discuss with potential clients the nature of the clients' current relationship with other service providers and the implications, including possible benefits or risks, of entering into a relationship with a new service provider.

(b) If a new client has been served by another agency or colleague, social workers should discuss with the client whether consultation with the previous service provider is in the client's best interest.

3.07 Administration

(a) Social work administrators should advocate within and outside their agencies for adequate resources to meet clients' needs.

(b) Social workers should advocate for resource allocation procedures that are open and fair. When not all clients' needs can be met, an allocation procedure should be developed that is nondiscriminatory and based on appropriate and consistently applied principles.

(c) Social workers who are administrators should take reasonable steps to ensure that adequate agency or organizational resources are available to provide appropriate staff supervision.

(d) Social work administrators should take reasonable steps to ensure that the working environment for which they are responsible is consistent with and encourages compliance with the *NASW Code of Ethics*. Social work administrators should take reasonable steps to eliminate any conditions in their organizations that violate, interfere with, or discourage compliance with the *Code*.

3.08 Continuing Education and Staff Development

Social work administrators and supervisors should take reasonable steps to provide or arrange for continuing education and staff development for all staff for whom they are responsible. Continuing education and staff development should address current knowledge and emerging developments related to social work practice and ethics.

3.09 Commitments to Employers

(a) Social workers generally should adhere to commitments made to employers and employing organizations.

(b) Social workers should work to improve employing agencies' policies and procedures and the efficiency and effectiveness of their services.

(c) Social workers should take reasonable steps to ensure that employers are aware of social workers' ethical obligations as set forth in the *NASW Code of Ethics* and of the implications of those obligations for social work practice.

(d) Social workers should not allow an employing organization's policies, procedures, regulations, or administrative orders to interfere with their ethical practice of social work. Social workers should take reasonable steps to ensure that their employing organizations' practices are consistent with the *NASW Code of Ethics*.

(e) Social workers should act to prevent and eliminate discrimination in the employing organization's work assignments and in its employment policies and practices.

(f) Social workers should accept employment or arrange student field placements only in organizations that exercise fair personnel practices.

(g) Social workers should be diligent stewards of the resources of their employing organizations, wisely conserving funds where appropriate and never misappropriating funds or using them for unintended purposes.

3.10 Labor-Management Disputes

(a) Social workers may engage in organized action, including the formation of and participation in labor unions, to improve services to clients and working conditions.

(b) The actions of social workers who are involved in labor-management disputes, job actions, or labor strikes should be guided by the profession's values, ethical principles, and ethical standards. Reasonable differences of opinion exist among social workers concerning their primary obligation as professionals during an actual or threatened labor strike or job action. Social workers should carefully examine relevant issues and their possible impact on clients before deciding on a course of action.

4. Social Workers' Ethical Responsibilities as Professionals

4.01 Competence

(a) Social workers should accept responsibility or employment only on the basis of existing competence or the intention to acquire the necessary competence.

(b) Social workers should strive to become and remain proficient in professional practice and the performance of professional functions. Social workers should critically examine and keep current with emerging knowledge relevant to social work. Social workers should routinely review the professional literature and participate in continuing education relevant to social work practice and social work ethics.

(c) Social workers should base practice on recognized knowledge, including empirically based knowledge, relevant to social work and social work ethics.

4.02 Discrimination

Social workers should not practice, condone, facilitate, or collaborate with any form of discrimination on the basis of race, ethnicity, national origin, color, sex, sexual orientation, age, marital status, political belief, religion, or mental or physical disability.

4.03 Private Conduct

Social workers should not permit their private conduct to interfere with their ability to fulfill their professional responsibilities.

4.04 Dishonesty, Fraud, and Deception

Social workers should not participate in, condone, or be associated with dishonesty, fraud, or deception.

4.05 Impairment

(a) Social workers should not allow their own personal problems, psychosocial distress, legal problems, substance abuse, or mental health difficulties to interfere with their professional judgment and performance or to jeopardize the best interests of people for whom they have a professional responsibility.

(b) Social workers whose personal problems, psychosocial distress, legal problems, substance abuse, or mental health difficulties interfere with their professional judgment and performance should immediately seek consultation and take appropriate remedial action by seeking professional help, making adjustments in workload, terminating practice, or taking any other steps necessary to protect clients and others.

4.06 Misrepresentation

(a) Social workers should make clear distinctions between statements made and actions engaged in as a private individual and as a representative of the social work profession, a professional social work organization, or the social worker's employing agency.

(b) Social workers who speak on behalf of professional social work organizations should accurately represent the official and authorized positions of the organizations.

(c) Social workers should ensure that their representations to clients, agencies, and the public of professional qualifications, credentials, education, competence, affiliations, services provided, or results to be achieved are accurate. Social workers should claim only those relevant professional credentials they actually possess and take steps to correct any inaccuracies or misrepresentations of their credentials by others.

4.07 Solicitations

(a) Social workers should not engage in uninvited solicitation of potential clients who, because of their circumstances, are vulnerable to undue influence, manipulation, or coercion.

(b) Social workers should not engage in solicitation of testimonial endorsements (including solicitation of consent to use a client's prior statement as a testimonial endorsement) from current clients or from other people who, because of their particular circumstances, are vulnerable to undue influence.

4.08 Acknowledging Credit

(a) Social workers should take responsibility and credit, including authorship credit, only for work they have actually performed and to which they have contributed.

(b) Social workers should honestly acknowledge the work of and the contributions made by others.

5. Social Workers' Ethical Responsibilities to the Social Work Profession

5.01 Integrity of the Profession

(a) Social workers should work toward the maintenance and promotion of high standards of practice.

(b) Social workers should uphold and advance the values, ethics, knowledge, and mission of the profession. Social workers should protect, enhance, and improve the integrity of the profession through appropriate study and research, active discussion, and responsible criticism of the profession.

(c) Social workers should contribute time and professional expertise to activities that promote respect for the value, integrity, and competence of the social work profession. These activities may include teaching, research, consultation, service, legislative testimony, presentations in the community, and participation in their professional organizations.

(d) Social workers should contribute to the knowledge base of social work and share with colleagues their knowledge related to practice, research, and ethics. Social workers should seek to con-tribute to the profession's literature and to share their knowledge at professional meetings and conferences.

(e) Social workers should act to prevent the unauthorized and unqualified practice of social work.

5.02 Evaluation and Research

(a) Social workers should monitor and evaluate policies, the implementation of programs, and practice interventions.

(b) Social workers should promote and facilitate evaluation and research to contribute to the development of knowledge.

(c) Social workers should critically examine and keep current with emerging knowledge relevant to social work and fully use evaluation and research evidence in their professional practice.

(d) Social workers engaged in evaluation or research should carefully consider possible consequences and should follow guidelines developed for the protection of evaluation and research participants. Appropriate institutional review boards should be consulted.

(e) Social workers engaged in evaluation or research should obtain voluntary and written informed consent from participants, when appropriate, without any implied or actual deprivation or penalty for refusal to participate; without undue inducement to participate; and with due regard for participants' well-being, privacy, and dignity. Informed consent should include information about the nature, extent, and duration of the participation requested and disclosure of the risks and benefits of participation in the research.

(f) When evaluation or research participants are incapable of giving informed consent, social workers should provide an appropriate explanation to the participants, obtain the participants' assent to the extent they are able, and obtain written consent from an appropriate proxy.

(g) Social workers should never design or conduct evaluation or research that does not use consent procedures, such as certain forms of naturalistic observation and archival research, unless rigorous and responsible review of the research has found it to be justified because of its prospective scientific, educational, or applied value and unless equally effective alternative procedures that do not involve waiver of consent are not feasible.

(h) Social workers should inform participants of their right to withdraw from evaluation and research at any time without penalty.

(i) Social workers should take appropriate steps to ensure that participants in evaluation and research have access to appropriate supportive services.

(j) Social workers engaged in evaluation or research should protect participants from unwarranted physical or mental distress, harm, danger, or deprivation.

(k) Social workers engaged in the evaluation of services should discuss collected information only for professional purposes and only with people professionally concerned with this information.

(l) Social workers engaged in evaluation or research should ensure the anonymity or confidentiality of participants and of the data obtained from them. Social workers should inform participants of any limits of confidentiality, the measures that will be taken to ensure confidentiality, and when any records containing research data will be destroyed.

(m) Social workers who report evaluation and research results should protect participants' confidentiality by omitting identifying information unless proper consent has been obtained authorizing disclosure.

(n) Social workers should report evaluation and research findings accurately. They should not fabricate or falsify results and should take steps to correct any errors later found in published data using standard publication methods.

(o) Social workers engaged in evaluation or research should be alert to and avoid conflicts of interest and dual relationships with participants, should inform participants when a real or potential conflict of interest arises, and should take steps to resolve the issue in a manner that makes participants' interests primary.

(p) Social workers should educate themselves, their students, and their colleagues about responsible research practices.

6. Social Workers' Ethical Responsibilities to the Broader Society

6.01 Social Welfare

Social workers should promote the general welfare of society, from local to global levels, and the development of people, their communities, and their environments. Social workers should advocate for living conditions conducive to the fulfillment of basic human needs and should promote social, economic, political, and cultural values and institutions that are compatible with the realization of social justice.

6.02 Public Participation

Social workers should facilitate informed participation by the public in shaping social policies and institutions.

6.03 Public Emergencies

Social workers should provide appropriate professional services in public emergencies to the greatest extent possible.

6.04 Social and Political Action

(a) Social workers should engage in social and political action that seeks to ensure that all people have equal access to the resources, employment, services, and opportunities they require to meet their basic human needs and to develop fully. Social workers should be aware of the impact of the political arena on practice and should advocate for changes in policy and legislation to improve social conditions in order to meet basic human needs and promote social justice.

(b) Social workers should act to expand choice and opportunity for all people, with special regard for vulnerable, disadvantaged, oppressed, and exploited people and groups.

(c) Social workers should promote conditions that encourage respect for cultural and social diversity within the United States and globally. Social workers should promote policies and practices that demonstrate respect for difference, support the expansion of cultural knowledge and resources, advocate for programs and institutions that demonstrate cultural competence, and promote policies that safeguard the rights of and confirm equity and social justice for all people.

(d) Social workers should act to prevent and eliminate domination of, exploitation of, and discrimination against any person, group, or class on the basis of race, ethnicity, national origin, color, sex, sexual orientation, age, marital status, political belief, religion, or mental or physical disability.

COUNSELOR LICENSURE BOARDS

Alabama	Alabama Board of Examiners in Marriage and Family Therapy 660 Adams Avenue, Suite ISO Montgomery, AL 36104 Phone: 334-269-9990 Fax: 334-263-6115 http://www.mft.state.al.us Alabama Board of Examiners in Counseling 950-22nd Street North, Suite 670 Birmingham, AL 35203 Phone: 205-458-8716, 800-822-3307 Fax: 205-822-3307 www.abec.state.al.us/
Alaska	Division of Occupational Licensing Board of Professional Counselors P.O. Box 110806 Juneau, AK 99877-0806 Phone: 907-465-2551 Fax: 907-465-2974 http: www.dced.state.ak.us/occ/ppco.htm
Arizona	Board of Behavioral Health Examiners 1400 West Washington, Room 350 Phoenix, AZ 85007 Phone: 602-542-1882 Fax: 602-542-1830 http://aspin.asu.edu/~azbbhe/
Arkansas	Board of Examiners of Counselor and Marriage- Family Therapist 124 Jackson Suite 312 McAlester 71753 Phone: 870-901-7055, 870-901-7059 Fax: 870-234-1842 http://www.accessarkansas.org/abec
California	Board of Behavioral Sciences 400 R. Street, Suite 3150 Sacramento, CA 95814-445-4933 Phone: 916-445-4933 Fax: 916-323-0707 http://www.bbs.ca.gov

COUNSELOR LICENSURE BOARDS

Colorado	Licensed Professional Counselor Examiner Board Mental Health Licensing Section 1560 Broadway, Suite 1370 Denver, CO 80202 Phone: 303-894-7766 Fax: 303-894-7747 http://www.dora.state.co.us/metal-health/staffdirectory.htm
Connecticut	Connecticut Licensed Professional Counselor, Dept. of Health 410 Capitol Avenue MS #12 APP P.O. Box 340308 Hartford, CT 06134-0308 Phone: 860-509-7590, 860-509-7591 Fax: 860-509-8457 www.dph.state.ct.us/
Delaware	Delaware Board of Professional Counselors of Mental Health 861 Silver Lake Blvd., Cannon Building # 203 Dover, DE 19904 Phone: 302-739-4522 Fax: 302-739-2711 http://professionallicensing.state.de.us/boards/profcounselors/index.shtml
Washington DC	Department of Health Board of Professional Counselors 825 North Capitol Street, NE 2nd Floor Phone: 202-442-4775 Fax: 202-442-9431 http://dchealth.dc.gov/prof_licensure/services/procoucomm.shtm
Florida	Florida Board of Clinical Social Worker, Marriage & Family Therapy & Mental Health Counseling Department of Health, Medical Quality Assurance 2020 Capitol Circle, SE, Bin# C08 Tallahassee, FL 32399-3250 Phone: 850-487-1129 Fax: 850-921-2569 www.doh.state.fl.us/mqa/491/491home.htm
Georgia	Georgia Composite Board of Professional Counselors,

COUNSELOR LICENSURE BOARDS

	Social Work and Family Therapy 166 Pryor Street, Southwest Atlanta, GA 30303 Phone: 404-656-3933 Fax: 404-651-9532 http://www.sos.state.ga.us/plb/counselors/
Hawaii	No Licensure
Idaho	Idaho State Counselor Licensure Board Bureau of Occupational Licenses 1109 Main Street, Suite 220 Boise, ID 83702-5642 Fax: 208-334-3945 http://www2.state.id.us/ibol/cou.htm
Illinois	Illinois Professional Counselor & Disciplinary Board 320 West Washington Street Springfield, IL 68786 Phone: 217-785-0822 Fax: 217-782-7645 www.nbcc.org/exams/stateboards.htm#ILLINOIS
Indiana	Indiana Social Work, Marriage and Family Health Counselor Board 402 West Washington St, Room 401 Indianapolis, IN 46204 Phone· 317-233-8789 Fax: 317-233-4236 http://www.in.gov/hpb/boards/mhcb/
Iowa	Iowa Board of Behavioral Science Examiners IA Dept of Public Health 321 East 12th Street Lucas Building 5th Floor Des Moines, IA 50319 Phone: 515-281-4413 Fax: 515-281-3121 Http://www.idph.state.ia.us/idph_pl/behavioral_science_index.html
Kansas	Kansas Behavioral Sciences Regulatory Board 712 South Kansas Avenue Topeka, KS 66603-3817 Phone: 913-296-3240 Fax: 913-296-3112

COUNSELOR LICENSURE BOARDS

	http://www.ink.org/public/bsrb
Kentucky	Kentucky Board of Professional Counselor Occupations and Professions, Perry Hall Annex 700 Louisville Road, Suite 2 Box 456 Frankfort, KY 40602 Phone: 502-564-3296 Fax: 502-696-1928 http://www.state.ky.us/agencies/finance/occupations/pro counselors/
Louisiana	Louisiana Licensed Professional Counselor Board of Examiners 8631 Summa Avenue, Suite A Baton Rouge, LA 70809 Phone: 225-765-2515 Fax: 225-765-2514 http://www.lpcboard.org/
Maine	Maine Board of Counseling Professionals 35 State House Station Augusta, ME 04333 Phone: 207-624-8626 Fax: 207-624-8637 http://www.state.me.us/pfr/olr/
Maryland	Board of Professional Counselors & Therapists MD Dept of Health and Mental Hygiene Metro Executive Center 4201 Patterson Avenue 3rd Floor Baltimore, MD 21215 Phone: 410-764-4732 Fax: 410-764-5987 http://www.dhmd.state.md.us/bopc/
Massachusetts	Board of Allied Mental Health & Human Service Professionals 239 Causeway Street Boston, MA 02114 Phone: 617-727-3080 Fax: 617-727-2366 http://www.cce-global.org/massexamsch.htm
Michigan	Michigan Board of Counseling P.O. Box 30670

COUNSELOR LICENSURE BOARDS

	Lansing, MI 48909 Phone: 517-335-0918 Fax: 517-373-3596 http:www.cis.state.mi.us/bhser/lic/boards/bdcouns.htm
Minnesota	No Licensure in Counseling
Mississippi	Mississippi Board of Examiners Licensed Professional Counselors 319 South Main Street Yahoo City. MS 39194 Phone: 1-888-860-7001 Fax: 662-751-4628 http://www.dmh.state.ms.us/profesional_licensure_and_certification.htm
Missouri	Missouri Committee for Professionals Counselors P.O. Box 1335 Jefferson City. MO 65102 Phone: 573-751-0018 Fax: 573-751-4176 www.ecodev.state.mo.us/pr/counselr/
Montana	Montana Professional & Occupational Licensing Division Board of Social Work Examiners & Professional Counselors 301 South Park, 4th Floor, P.O. Box 200513 Helana, MT 59620-0513 Phone: 406-841-2369 Fax: 406-841-2305 www.discoveringmontana.com/dli.swp
Nebraska	Nebraska Board of Examiners in Professional Counseling 301 Centennial Mall South, P.O. Box 95007 Lincoln, NE 68509-5007 Phone: 402-471-2115 Fax: 402-471-0380 http://www.dol.state.ne.us/nwd/workserv/jobcareer/data pubs/occupations/lco/nlo.htm

COUNSELOR LICENSURE BOARDS

Nevada	Board of Marriage & Family Therapist Examiners P.O. Box 72758 Las Vegas, NV 89170 Phone: 702-486-7388 Fax: 702-486-7258 http://marriage.state.nv.us/ (Under construction) Board of Examiners for Alcohol and Drug Abuse Counselors 440 Dayton Valley RD, Suite B Dayton Nevada 89403 Phone: 775-246-2260 Fax: 775-246-2262 http://alcohol.state.nv.us/Contact.htm
New Hampshire	New Hampshire Board of Examiners in Psychology & Mental Health Practice 49 Donovan Street Concord, NH 03301 Phone: 603-271-6762 Fax: 603-271-3950 http://webster.state.nh.us/mhpb/
New Jersey	Board of Marriage and Family Therapy Examiners Division of Consumer Affairs 124 Halsey Street P.O. Box 45007, Newark, NJ 07101 Phone: 973-504-6415 Fax: 973-648-3536 http://www.state.nj.us/lps/ca/brief/marcon.htm
New Mexico	Counselor & Therapy Practice Board 2055 Pacheco Street, Suite 300 Santa Fe, NM 87504 Phone: 505-476-7100 Fax: 505-827-7085 http://www.rld.state.nm.us/b&c/counseling/counselingth erapypracticeboard.htm
New York	Licensure legislation was introduced in the NY state legislature but did not pass in 1999-2000. For further information on NY licensure issues only, contact: Judith Ritterman, President - NY Mental Health

COUNSELOR LICENSURE BOARDS

	Counselors - E-mail: JRitter102@aol.com Tel: 516-472-9616; Fax: 516-472-2402 Website: www.legislativeaction.homestead.com/index.html
North Carolina	North Carolina Board of Licensed Professional Counselors P.O. Box 21005 Raleigh, NC 27619-1005 Phone: 919-787-1980 Fax: 919-571-8672 www.NCBLPC.org
North Dakota	North Dakota Board of Counselor Examiners 2112 10th Ave SE Mandan, ND 58554 Phone: 701-667-5969 Fax: 701-667-5969 http://www.sendit.nodak.edu/ndbce/
Ohio	Ohio Counselor & Social Work Board 77 S. High Street 16th Floor Columbus, OH 43266-0340 Phone: 614-752-5161 Fax: 614-644-8112 http://www.state.oh.us/csw/
Oklahoma	Oklahoma LPC Committee 1000 NE 10th St. Oklahoma City, OK 73117-1299 Phone: 405-271-6030 Fax: 405-271-1918 www.health.state.ok.us/program/lpc/
Oregon	Oregon Board of Licensed Professional Counselors & Therapists 3218 Pringle Rd SE #160 Salem, OR 97302-6312 Phone: 503-378-5499 Fax: Not Listed on Website http://www.oblpct.state.or.us/
Pennsylvania	Clara Flinchum, Board Administrator State Board of Social Workers, Marriage and Family Therapists, and Professional Counselors

COUNSELOR LICENSURE BOARDS

	PO BOX 2649 Harrisburg, PA 17105 Phone: 717-783-1389 Fax 717-787-7769 http://www.dos.state.pa.us/bpoa/cwp/view.asp?a=1104& q=433177
Rhode Island	Rhode Island Board of Mental Health Counselors and Marriage and Family Therapists Capitol Health Cannon Building #104 Providence, RI 02908-5097 Phone: 401-277-2827, ext 106 Fax: 401-277-1272 http://www.healthri.org/hsr/professions/mf_counsel.htm
South Carolina	South Carolina Board of Examiners for LPC, AC, MFT P.O. BOX 11329 Columbia, SC 29211-1329 Phone: 803-896-4660 Fax: 803-734-4218 www.llr.sc.edu/bel.htm
South Dakota	South Dakota Board of Counselor Examiners P.O. BOX 1822, 1116 S. Minnesota Ave Sioux Falls, SD 57101-1822 Phone: 605-331-2927 Fax: 605-331-2043 www.state.sd.us/dcr/counselor
Tennessee	Tennessee Board of Professional Counselors & MFTS 1st Fl Cordell Hull Bldg, 426 5th Avenue North Nashville, TN 37247-1010 Phone: 615-532-3202, 888-310-4650 Fax: 615-532-5164 http://www2.state.tn.us/health/Boards/PC_MFT&CPT/
Texas	Texas State Board of Examiners of Professional Counselors 1100 West 49th St Austin, TX 78756-3183 Phone: 512-834-6658 Fax: 512-834-6789 http://www.tdh.state.tx.us/hcqs/plc/lpc/lpc_def.htm
Utah	Utah Professional Counselor Licensing Board 160 East 300 South 4th Fl, P.O. BOX 45802

COUNSELOR LICENSURE BOARDS

	Salt Lake City, UT 84145 Phone: 801-530-6628 Fax: 801-530-6511 http://www.dopl.utah.gov/licensing/professional_counsel or.html
Vermont	Vermont Board of Allied Mental Health Practitioners Office of Professional Regulations Secretary of State's Office Red Stone Bldg. 26 Terrace Street, Drawer 09 Montpelier, VT 05609-1106 Phone: 802-828-2390 Fax: 802-828-2496 http://www.state.vt.us/
Virginia	Virginia Board of Counseling Dept. of Health Professionals 6606 W. Broad St 4th Floor Richmond, VA 23230-1717 Phone: 804-662-9912 Fax: 804-662-7250 http://www.dhp.state.va.us/counseling/default.htm
Washington	Washington State Department of Health Counselor Programs P.O. 47869 Olympia, WA 98504-7869 Phone: 360-664-9098 Fax: 360-586-7774 http://www.doh.wa.gov/hsqa/hpqad/coun/default.htm#w elcome
West Virginia	West Virginia Board of Examiners in Counseling Post Office Box 129 Ona, West Virginia 25545 Phone: 800-520-3852, 304-767-3061; Fax: 304-767-3062 http://www.state.wv.us/wvbec/
Wisconsin	Wisconsin Examining Board of Social Work, Marriage, Family Therapists and Professional Counselors P.O. BOX 8935 Madison, WI 53709-8935 Phone: 608-267-7223

COUNSELOR LICENSURE BOARDS

	Fax: 608-267-0644 http://www.drl.state.wi.us/
Wyoming	Wyoming Professional Counselors and M&F Therapists 2301 Central Ave Cheyenne, WY 82002 Phone: 307-777-7788 Fax: 307-777-3508 http://soswy.state.wy.us/director/ag-bd/mental.htm

PSYCHOLOGIST LICENSURE BOARDS

Alabama	Alabama Board of Examiners in Psychology 660 Adams Avenue Suite 360 Montgomery, Alabama 36104 Phone: 334-242-4127 Fax: Not Listed on Website (Email only: albdpsychology@mindspring.com) http://psychology.state.al.us/
Alaska	Board of Psychologist and Psychological Associate Examiners P.O. Box 110806 Juneau, AK 99811-0806 Phone: 907-465-3811 Fax: 907-465-2974 http://www.dced.state.ak.us/occ/ppsy.htm
Arizona	Arizona Board of Psychologist Examiners 1400 West Washington, Room 235 Phoenix, AZ 85007 Phone: 602-542-8161 Fax: 602-542-8279 http://www.psychologyinfo.com/directory/AZ/boa rd.html
Arkansas	Arkansas Board of Examiners in Psychology 101 East Capitol, Suite 415 Little Rock, AR 72201 Phone: 501-682-6167 Fax: 501-682-6165 http://www.state.ar.us/abep/
California	California Board of Psychology 1422 Howe Avenue, Suite 22 Sacramento, CA 95625-3200 Phone: 916-263-2699 Fax: 916-263-2699 http://www.psychboard.ca.gov/
Colorado	State of Colorado Mental Health Licensing Section 1560 Broadway, Suite 1370

PSYCHOLOGIST LICENSURE BOARDS

	Denver, CO 8020 Phone: 303-894-7766 Fax: 303-894-7747 http://www.dora.state.co.us/mental-health/
Connecticut	Connecticut Board of Examiners of Psychologists Department of Public Health 410 Capitol Avenue, MS# 12APP P.O. Box 340308 Hartford, CT 06134 Phone: 860-509-7567, 860-509-8000 Fax: 860-509-7539 (Regulatory Services) www.dph.state.ct.us/
Delaware	State of Delaware Department of Administrative Services Division of Professional Regulation Cannon Building 861 Silver Lake Blvd. Suite 203 Dover, DE 19904-2467 Phone: 302-744-4500 Fax: 302-739-2711 http://professionallicensing.state.de.us/boards/psychology/faqs.shtml
Washington D.C.	Department of Health Board of Psychology 825 North Capitol Street, NE, 2nd Floor Washington, DC 20002 Phone: 202-442-4764 Fax: 202-442-9431 http://dchealth.dc.gov/prof_license/services/boards_main_action.asp?strAppId=22
Florida	Florida Board of Psychology 4052 Bald Cypress Way, BIN C05 Tallahassee, FL 32399-3255 Phone: 850-245-4373 Fax: Not Listed on Website Email only: MQA_Psychology@doh.state.fl.us http://www.doh.state.fl.us/mqa/psychology/2001_py_home.html

PSYCHOLOGIST LICENSURE BOARDS

Georgia	Georgia State Board of Examiners 237 Coliseum Drive Macon, Georgia 31217 Phone: 312-207-1670 Fax: 478-207-1300 http://www.sos.state.ga.us/acrobat/ExamBoards/Psychology/app_2002.pdf
Hawaii	Hawaii Board Psychology Department of Commerce and Consumer Affairs P.O. Box 3469 Honolulu, HI 96801 Phone: 808-586-2693 Fax: Not Listed on Website Email only: psychology@dcca.state.hi.us http://www.state.hi.us/dcca/pvl/
Idaho	The Idaho State Board of Psychologist Examiners 1109 Main Street, Suite 220 Boise, Idaho 83702-5641 Phone: 208-334-3233 Fax: 208-334-3945 http://www2.state.id.us/ibol/psy.html
Illinois	Illinois Department of Professional Regulation- Psychology Springfield Office: 320 West Washington Springfield, IL 62786 Phone: 217-785-0800 Fax: 217-782-7645 http://www.dpr.state.il.us/WHO/Psych.asp
Illinois (cont)	Chicago Office: James R. Thompson Center 100 West Randolph Suite 9-300 Chicago, IL 60601 Phone: 312-814-4500 Fax: Not Listed on Website http://www.dpr.state.il.us/WHO/Psych.asp

PSYCHOLOGIST LICENSURE BOARDS

Indiana	Indiana State Psychology Board 402 W. Washington St, Room 041 Indianapolis, IN 46204 Phone: 317-232-1129 Fax: 317-233-4236 http://www.in.gov/hpb/boards/ispb/
Iowa	Iowa Bureau of Professional Licensure Psychology Board Level B Hoover Building Des Moines, IA 50319-0001 Phone: 515-281-5703 Fax: 515-281-6137 http://www.state.ia.us/idph_pl/psychology/index.htm
Kansas	Behavioral Sciences Regulatory Board 712 S. Kansas Ave Topeka, KS 66603-3817 Phone: 785-296-3240 Fax: 785-296-3112 http://www.ksbsrb.org/psychologists.html
Kentucky	Kentucky Board of Examiners P.O. Box 1360 Frankfort, KY 40602 Phone: 502-564-9296 ex225 Fax: 502-696-1923 http://www.state.ky.us/agencies/finance/boards/psychology/index.htm
Louisiana	Louisiana State Board of Examiners of Psychologists 8280 YMCA Plaza One Oak Square, Building 8B Baton Rouge, LA 70810 Phone: 225-763-3935 Fax: 225-763-3968 http://www.lsbep.org/
Maine	Maine Department of Professional and Financial Regulation

PSYCHOLOGIST LICENSURE BOARDS

	Office of Licensing & Registration # 35 State House Station Augusta, Maine 0433-0035 Phone: 207-624-8603 Fax: 207-624-8637 http://www.state.me.us/pfr/olr/about.htm
Maryland	Maryland Board of Examiners of Psychologists 4201 Patterson Avenue Baltimore, MD 21215-2299 Phone: 410-764-4787 Fax: 410-358-7896 http://www.marylandpsychology.org/section.cfm?sectionid=14
Massachusetts	Board of Registration of Psychologists 239 Causeway Street, Suite 500 Boston, MA 02114 Phone: 617-727-3074 Fax: 617-727-2197 http://www.state.ma.us/reg/boards/py/default.htm
Michigan	Michigan Board of Psychology 611 West Ottawa Lansing, MI 48909 Phone: 517-373-9102 Fax: 517-322-1356 http://www.cis.state.mi.us/bhser/lic/home.html
Minnesota	Minnesota Board of Psychology 2829 University Avenue SE, Suite 320 St. Paul, MN 55414-3237 Phone: 612-617-2230 Fax: Not Listed on Website Email only: psychology.board@state.mn.us http://www.psychologyinfo.com/directory/MN/board.html
Mississippi	Mississippi State Board of Psychological Examiners 812 North President Street Jackson, MS 39202-2560

PSYCHOLOGIST LICENSURE BOARDS

	Phone: 601-353-8871 Fax: 601-268-0296 (coordinator) http://www.mpassoc.org/mpa-info3.html
Missouri	State Committee of Psychologists 3605 Missouri Blvd P.O. Box 1335 Jefferson City, MO 65102-1335 Phone: 573-751-0099 Fax: 573-526-3489 http://www.ded.state.mo.us/regulatorylicensing/professionalregistration/psych/
Montana	Montana Board of Psychologists 111 N. Last Chance Gulch Arcade Building, Lower Level P.O. Box 200513 Helena, MT 59620-0513 Phone: 406-444-5436 Fax: Not Listed on Website http://www.discoveringmontana.com/dli/bsd/license/map.htm
North Carolina	North Carolina Psychology Board 895 State Farm Road, Suite 101 Boone, NC 29607 Phone: 828-262-2258 Fax: 828-265-8611 http://www.ncpsychologyboard.org/
Nevada	State of Nevada Board of Psychological Examiners P.O. Box 2286 Reno, NV 89505-2286 Phone: 775-688-1268 Fax: 775-688-1272 http://psyexam.state.nv.us/
Nebraska	Nebraska Health and Human Services System Department of HHS Regulation and Licensure P.O. Box 95007

PSYCHOLOGIST LICENSURE BOARDS

	Lincoln, NE 68509-5007 Phone: 402-471-2113 Fax: 402-471-3577 http://www.hhs.state.ne.us/crl/mhcs.htm
New Hampshire	New Hampshire Board of Mental Health Practice 49 Donovan Street Concord, NH 03301 Phone: 603-271-6762 Fax: Not Listed on Website http://www.state.nh.us/mhpb/index.html
New Jersey	New Jersey Department of Law and Public Safety Division of Community Affairs Board of Psychological Examiners PO Box 45017 Newark, NJ 0701 Phone: 973-504-6470 Fax: 973-648-3536 http://www.state.nj.us/lps/ca/psy/psydir.htm
New York	New York State Board for Psychology NYS Education Dept. Cultural Education Center Room 3041 Albany, NY 12230 Phone: 518-474-3866 Fax: 518-474-1449 http://www.op.nysed.gov/psych.htm
North Dakota	North Dakota State Board of Psychologists Examiners P.O. Box 9830 Grand Forks, ND 85202 Phone: 701-777-3792 Fax: 701-777-3454 http://www.governor.state.nd.us/boards/boards-query.asp?Board_ID=88
Ohio	State Board of Psychology 77 South High Street, 18th Floor Columbus, Ohio 43266-0321 Phone: 614-466-8008

PSYCHOLOGIST LICENSURE BOARDS

	Fax: 614-644-9176 http://www.state.oh.us/psy
Oklahoma	Oklahoma Psychological Association 601 N. W. Grand Blvd, Suite C Oklahoma City, OK 73118-6032 Phone: 405-879-0069 Fax: 405-879-0304 http://okpsych.org/
Oregon	Oregon Board of Psychologist Examiners 3218 Pringle Road SE, Suite 130 Salem, OR 97302-6309 Phone: 503-378-4154 Fax: 503-378-3575 http://www.obpe.state.or.us/staff_board.htm#conta ct
Pennsylvania	State Board of Psychology P.O. Box 2649 Harrisburg, PA 17105-2649 Phone 717-783-7155 Fax 717-787-7769 http://www.dos.state.pa.us/bpoa/cwp/view.asp?a= 1104&q=433051
Rhode Island	Rhode Island Department of Health Division of Health Services Regulation Health Professions 3 Capitol Hill- Room 104 Providence, RI 02902 Phone: 401-222-1272 Fax: 401-222-1272 http://www.health.state.ri.us/
South Carolina	Board of Examiners in Psychology Synergy Business Park Kingstree Building 110 Centerview Dr. Suite 306 Columbia, SC 29210 Phone 803-896-4664

PSYCHOLOGIST LICENSURE BOARDS

	Fax 803-896- 4687 http://www.llr.state.sc.us/POL/Psychology/INDEX.ASP
South Dakota	South Dakota Department of Commerce and Regulation 135 East Illinois, Suite 214 Spearfish, SD 57783 Phone: 605-642-1600 Fax: 605-642-1756 http://www.state.sd.us/dcr/psychologists/
Tennessee	Tennessee Department of Health 425 5th Avenue N. Nashville, TN 37247 Phone: 615-741-3111 Fax: 315-741-2491 http://www.state.tn.us/health/
Utah	Division of Occupational and Professional Licensing 160 East 300 South Salt Lake City, Utah Phone: 801-530-6628 Fax: 801-530- 6511 http://www.dopl.utah.gov/
Vermont	Vermont Board of Psychological Examiners P.O. Box 1017 100 State Street- Suite 330 Montpelier, VT 05601-1017 Phone: 802-229-5447 Fax: 802-229-5003 http://www.central-vt.com/web/vpa/examiner.htm
Virginia	Virginia Board of Psychology 6606 West Broad Street, 4th Floor Richmond, VA 23230-1717 Phone: 804-662-9913 Fax: 804-662-7250 http://www.dhp.state.va.us/psychology/default.htm

PSYCHOLOGIST LICENSURE BOARDS

Washington	Washington State Board of Psychology Health Professions Quality Assurance 1300 SE Quince Street, PO Box 47860 Olympia, Washington 98504-7860 Phone: 360-236-4700 Fax: 360-236-4818 https://wws2.wa.gov/doh/hpqa-licensing/Contact_info/CSCpopup.htm
West Virginia	West Virginia Board of Examiners of Psychologists P.O. Box 3955 Charleston, WV 25339-3955 Phone: 304-558-0604 Fax: Not Listed Not yet posted on the Web
Wisconsin	Wisconsin Psychology Examining Board Department of Regulation and Licensing P.O. Box 8935 Madison, WI 59708-8935 Phone: 608-266-0145 Fax: 608-267-6044 http://www.drl.state.wi.us/
Wyoming	Wyoming State Board of Psychology 2020 Carey Avenue, #201 Cheyenne, WY 82002 Phone: 307-777-6529 Fax: 307-777-3508 http://soswy.state.wy.us/director/ag-bd/psych.htm

SOCIAL WORK LICENSURE BOARDS

Alabama	State Board of Social Work Examiners Folsom Administrative Building 64 North Union Street, Suite 129 Montgomery, AL 36130 Phone: 334-242-5860, 205-242-5860 Fax: 334-242-0280 http://abswe.state.al.us/
Alaska	Department of Commerce & Economic Development Board of Clinical Social Work Examiners P.O. Box 110806 Juneau, AK 99811-0806 Phone: 907-465-2551 Fax: 907-465-2974 http://www.dced.state.ak.us/occ/pcsw.htm
Arizona	Board of Behavioral Health Examiners 1400 West Washington, #350 Phoenix, AZ 85007 Phone: 602-542-1882 Fax: 602-542-1830 http://aspin.asu.edu/~azbbhe/
Arkansas	Social Work Licensing Board 2020 West Third, Suite 503 P.O. Box 250381 Little Rock, Arkansas 72225 Phone: 501-372-5071 Fax: 501-372-6301 http://www.state.ar.us/swlb/
California	Board of Behavioral Sciences 400 R. Street, RM 3150 Sacramento, CA 95814 Phone: 916-445-4933 Fax: 916-323-0707 http://www.bbs.ca.gov/
Colorado	Board of Social Work Examiners 1560 Broadway, Suite 1340 Denver, CO 80202 Phone: 303-894-7766

SOCIAL WORK LICENSURE BOARDS

	Fax: 303-894-7747 http://www.dora.state.co.us/mental-health/swboard.htm
Connecticut	Department of Public Health Clinical Social Worker Licensure 410 Capitol Avenue, MS #12APP Hartford, CT 06134 Phone: 860-509-7567 Fax: Not Listed on Website (No direct Email) www.dph.state.ct.us/
Delaware	Board of Clinical Social Work Examiners Cannon Building, Suite 203 861 Silverlake Boulevard Dover, DE 19904 Phone: 302-703-4522 x220 Fax: 302-739-2711, 302-739-4522 http://professionallicensing.state.de.us/boards/socialwor kers/index.shtml
Washington D.C.	Board of Social Work 614 H. Street, NW, Room 904 Washington, DC 20001 Phone: 202-442-5888 Fax: 202-727-7662 777.dcra.org/opla.shtm
Florida	Board of Clinical Social Work, Marriage, & Family Therapy, & Mental Health Counseling 2020 Capitol Circle, SE Bin #C08 Tallahassee, FL 32399-3258 Phone: 850-488-0595 Fax: 850-921-5389 www.doh.state.fl.us/491/soc_home.html
Georgia	Composite Board of Professional Counselor, Social Workers and Marriage And Family Therapists 237 Coliseum Drive Macon, GA 31217-3858

SOCIAL WORK LICENSURE BOARDS

	Phone: 912-207-1670 Fax: 478-207-1363 http://www.sos.state.ga.us/plb/counselors/
Hawaii	Department of Commerce & Consumer Affairs Social Work Program P.O. Box 3469 Honolulu, HI 96813 Phone: 808-586-3000 Fax: Not Listed on Website (Email only) Email: social_worker@dcca.state.hi.us http://www.state.hi.us/dcca/pvl/areas_social_worker.htm l
Idaho	State Board of Social Work Examiners Bureau of Occupational Licensing Owyhee, Plaza/ 1109 Main St Suite 220 Boise, ID 83702 Phone: 208-334-3233 Fax: 208-342-4666 http://www2.state.id.us/ibol/swo.htm
Indiana	Social Work Certification and Marriage & Family Therapists Credentialing Board Health Professions Bureau/ IN Government Center 402 West Washington Street, Room 041 Indianapolis, IN 46204 Phone: 317-234-2064 Fax: 317-233-4236 http://www.in.gov/hpb/boards/mhcb/
Illinois	SW Examining & Disciplinary Board Department of Professional Regulation 320 West Washington Street, 3rd Floor Springfield, IL 62786 Phone: 217-785-0800 Fax: 217-782-7645 www.dpr.state.il.us/WHO/sw.asp
Iowa	Board of Social Work Examiners

SOCIAL WORK LICENSURE BOARDS

	Bureau of Professional Licensure Lucas State Office Building 321 E. 12th Street Des Moines, IA 50319-0075 Phone: 515-281-4422 Fax: 515-281-3121 http://www.idph.state.ia.us/idph_pl/social_work_index.html
Kansas	Kansas Behavioral Sciences Regulatory Board 712 S. Kansas Avenue Topeka, KS 66603 Phone: 785- 296-3240, 913-296-3240 Fax: 785-296-3112 http://www.ksbsrb.org/social-workers.html
Kentucky	Board of Examiners of Social Work Berry Hill Annex Louisville Road, Box 456 Frankfort, KY 40602 Phone: 502- 564-3296, Ext. 230 Fax: 502-696-1931 http://www.state.ky.us/agencies/finance/occupations/socialwork/
Louisiana	State Board of Board Certified Social Work Examiners 11930 Perkins Road, Suite B Baton Rouge, LA 70810 Phone: 225-763-3470 Fax: 225-756-3472 http://www.labswe.org/
Maine	State Board of Social Work Licensure 35 State House Station Augusta, Maine 04333 Phone: 207-624-8609 Fax: 207-624-8637 http://www.state.me.us/pfr/olr/categories/cat40.htm
	State Board of Social Work Examiners Department of Health & Mental Hygiene

SOCIAL WORK LICENSURE BOARDS

Maryland	4201 Patterson Drive Baltimore, MD 21215-2299 Phone: 410- 764-4788 Fax: 410-358-2469 http://www.dhmh.state.md.us/bswe/
Massachusetts	The Board of Registration of Social Workers 239 Causeway Street, Suite 500 Boston, MA 02114 Phone 617-727-3074 Fax 617-727-2197 http://www.state.ma.us/reg/boards/sw/default.htm
Michigan	Board of Examiners of Social Work P.O. Box 30246 Lansing, MI 48909 Phone: 517- 241-9245, 517-373-1653 Fax: 517-373-2179 http://www.cis.state.mi.us/bhser/lic/home.htm
Minnesota	Board of Social Work 2829 University Ave, SE Suite 340 Saint Paul, MN 55414-3239 Phone: 612-617-2100 Fax: 612-617-2103 http://www.socialwork.state.mn.us/
Mississippi	Board of Examiners for Social Workers and Marriage & Family Therapists P.O. Box 4508 Jackson, MS 39215-4508 Phone: 601-987-6806 Fax: 601-987-6808 http://www.msboeswmft.com/
Missouri	Division of Professional Registration State Committee for Social Workers P.O. Box 1335 Jefferson City, MO 65102-1335 Phone: 573-751-0885 Fax: 573-751-0890 http://www.ded.state.mo.us/regulatorylicensing/professi

SOCIAL WORK LICENSURE BOARDS

	onalregistration/social/index.html
Montana	Board of Social Work Examiners 111 North Jackson, Arcade Building P.O. Box 200513 Helena, MT 59620-0407 Phone: 406- 841-2369 Fax: 406-841- 2305 http://www.discoveringmontana.com/dli/bsd/license/bsd_boards/swp_board/board_page.htm
Nebraska	Bureau of Examining Boards 301 Centennial Mall South P.O. Box 94986 Lincoln, Nebraska 68509-4986 Phone: 402- 471-2117 Fax: 402-471-3577 http://www.hhs.state.ne.us/crl/mhcs.htm
Nevada	Board of Examiners for Social Workers 4600 Kietzke lane, Suite C121 Reno, NV 89502 Phone: 775-688-2555 Fax: Not Listed (Requests Via Website) http://socwork.state.nv.us/ (website under construction)
New Hampshire	Board of Mental Health Practice 105 Pleasant Street Concord, NH 03301 Phone: 603- 271-6762 Fax: Not Listed on Website http://www.state.nh.us/mhpb/
New Jersey	State Board of Social Work Examiners 124 Haley Street, 6th Floor P.O. Box 45033 Newark, New Jersey 07101 Phone: 973- 504-6495 Fax: 973-273-8067 http://www.state.nj.us/lps/ca/social/swlic.htm
New York	State Board of Social Work

SOCIAL WORK LICENSURE BOARDS

	NY State Education Department Cultural Education Center, RM #3041 Albany, NY 12230 Phone: 518-474-4974, 800-342-3729 Fax: 540-829-0142 http://www.op.nysed.gov/csw.htm
North Carolina	Certification Board for Social Work 130 South Church Street P.O. Box 1043 Asheboro, NC 27204 Phone: 336-625-1679 Fax: 336-625-1680 http://www.nccbsw.org/
North Dakota	Board of Social Work Examiners P.O. Box 914 Bismarck, ND 58502-0914 Phone: 701-222-0255 Fax: 701-224-9824 http://www.ndbswe.com/
Ohio	Social Work Board 77 South High Street, 16th Floor Columbus, OH 43266-0340 Phone: 614- 466-0912 Fax: 614-728-7790 http://www.state.oh.us/csw/
Oklahoma	Board of Licensed Social Workers 3535 NW 58th, Suite 765 Oklahoma City, OK 73112 Phone: 405- 946-7230 Fax: 405-942-1070 http://www.state.ok.us/~osblsw/
Oregon	State Board of Licensed Clinical Social Workers 3218 Pringle Road, SE, Suite 240 Salem, OR 93702-6310 Phone: 503-378-5735 Fax: 503-385-4465 http://bcsw.state.or.us/

SOCIAL WORK LICENSURE BOARDS

Pennsylvania	State Board of Social Workers, Marriage & Family Therapists and Professional Counselors P.O. Box 2629 Harrisburg, PA 17105-2649 Phone 717-783-1389 Fax 717-787-7769 http://www.dos.state.pa.us/bpoa/cwp/view.asp?a=1104& q=433177
Rhode Island	Division of Professional Regulation Rhode Island Department of Health 3 Capitol Hill, Room 104 Providence, RI 02908-5097 Phone: 401-277-2827 Fax: 401-222-1272 http://www.healthri.org/hsr/professions/s_work.htm
South Carolina	Board of Social Work Examiners P.O. Box 11329 Columbia, SC 29211-1329 Phone 803-896-4665 Fax: 803-896-4687 http://www.llr.state.sc.us/POL/SocialWorkers/Default.ht m
South Dakota	Board of Social Work Examiners 135 East Illinois, Suite 214 Spearfish, SD 57783 Phone: 609- 642-1600 Fax: 605-642-1756 http://www.state.sd.us/dcr/socialwork/soc-hom.htm
Tennessee	Board of SW Certification & Licensure Cordell Hull Building 425 5th Avenue, North Nashville, TN 37247-1010 Phone: 615-532-5132 Fax: 615-532-5164 www.state.tn.us/health/Boards/SW/index.htm

SOCIAL WORK LICENSURE BOARDS

Texas	State Board of Social Work Examiners 1100 West 49th Street Austin, TX 78756-3183 Phone: 512- 719-3521, 512-450-3255 Fax: 512-834-6677 http://www.tdh.state.tx.us/hcqs/plc/lsw/lsw_default.htm
Utah	Division of Occupational and Professional Licensing P.O. Box 146701 Salt Lake City, UT 84114-6701 Phone 866-275-3675 Fax 801-530- 6511 http://www.dopl.utah.gov/
Vermont	Office of the Secretary of State Licensing and Registration Division 109 State Street Montpelier, VT 05609 Phone: 828-2390 Fax: Not Listed on Website Email: dlafaill@sec.state.vt.us http://vtprofessionals.org/opr1/social_workers
Virginia	Board of Social Work 6606 West Broad Street, 4th Floor Richmond, VA 23230-1717 Phone: 804- 662-9914 Fax: 804-662-7250 http://www.dhp.state.va.us/social/default.htm
Washington	Washington State Board of Psychology Health Professions Quality Assurance 1300 SE Quince Street, PO Box 47860 Olympia, Washington 98504-7860 Phone: 360-236-4700 Fax: 360-236-4818 https://wws2.wa.gov/doh/hpqa- licensing/Contact_info/CSCp
West Virginia	Board of Social Work Examiners P.O. Box 5459 Charleston, West Virginia 25361

SOCIAL WORK LICENSURE BOARDS

	Phone: 304- 558-8816 Fax: 304-558-4189 http://www.state.wv.us/socialworkboard/
Wisconsin	Board of Social Workers, Marriage and Family Therapists, and Professional Counselors Department of Regulation and Licensing P.O. Box 8935 Madison, WI 53708-8935 Phone: 608- 267-7212 Fax: Not Listed (Email only) Email: web@drl.state.wi.us http://www.drl.state.wi.us/
Wyoming	Mental Health Professions Licensing Board 202 Carey Ave., Suite 201 Cheyenne, WY 82002 Phone: 307-777-7788, 307-777-6313 Fax: 307 777-3508 http://soswy.state.wy.us/director/ag-bd/mental.htm

Appendix C

Mental Health Acronyms

AASCB   American Association of State Counseling Boards

ABA   Applied Behavioral Analysis

ADA   Americans with Disabilities Act

ADD   Attention Deficit Disorder

ADHD   Attention Deficit Hyperactivity Disorder

APE   Adaptive Physical Education

AT   Assistive Technology

APS   Approved Private School

ARC   Association for Retarded Citizens

AS   Asperger's Syndrome

CACREP   Council for Accreditation of Counseling and Related
               Educational Programs

CBA   Curriculum Based Assessment

CCMHC   Certified Clinical Mental Health Counselor

CER   Comprehensive Evaluation Report

CFR   Code of Federal Regulations

CORE   Council on Rehabilitation Education

CRC   Certified Rehabilitation Counselor

CRCC   Commission on Rehabilitation Counselor Certification

CRCE	Certified Rehabilitation Counselor Examination
DTT	Discrete Trial Training
ED	Emotional Disturbance
EI	Early Intervention
ELC	Education Law Center
EMR	Educable Mentally Retarded
ES	Emotional Support
ES	English as a Second Language
ESY	Extended School Year
FAPE	Free and Appropriate Public Education
FAS	Fetal Alcohol Syndrome
FBA	Functional Behavioral Assessment
HCEFP	Handicapped Children's Early Education Program
IDEA	Individuals with Disabilities Education Act
IEP	Individualized Education Program
IFSP	Individualized Family Service Plan
IQ	Intelligence Quotient
IS	Instructional Support
IST	Instructional Support Team/Teacher
LD	Learning Disability
LEP	Limited English Proficiency

LRE	Least Restrictive Environment
MA	Medical Assistance
MDE	Multi-Disciplinary Evaluation
MDT	Multi-Disciplinary Team
MH	Mental Health
MR	Mental Retardation
NBCC	National Board for Certified Counselors
NCE	National Counselor Examination
NCMHCE	National Clinical Mental Health Counselor Examination
NEP	Non-English Proficiency
NORA	Notice of Recommended Action
ODD	Oppositional Defiant Disorder
ODR	Office of Dispute Resolution
OHI	Other Health Impairment
OSE	Office of Special Education
OT	Occupational Therapy
PDD	Pervasive Development Disorder
PDD-NOS	Pervasive Developmental Disorder Not Otherwise Specified
PT	Physical Therapy
SDI	Specially Designed Instruction

SED	Serious Emotional Disturbance/Seriously Emotionally Disturbed
SEED	Special Education Early Development
SID	Sensory Integration Dysfunction
S/L	Speech and Language
SLD	Specific Learning Disability
TMR	Trainable Mentally Retarded
VWA	Victim Witness Advocacy
VEU	Victim Witness Unit
WIAT	Wechsler Individual Achievement Test
WISC	Wechsler Intelligence Test

Appendix D

Online Professional Associations and Organizations in Mental Health

American Association for Geriatric Psychiatry
www.aagpgpa.org

American Association for Marriage and Family Therapy
www.aamft.org

American Association for Psychology and the Performing Arts
http://members.tripod.com/~SRB123/AAPA.html

American Association for Therapeutic Humor
http://ideanurse.com/aath

American Association of Pastoral Counselors
www.aapc.org

American Association of Psychotherapists
www.angelfire.com

American Association of Suicidology
www.cyberpsych.org

American Association on Mental Retardation
www.aamr.org

American Counseling Association
www.aca.org

American Dance Therapy Association
www.ADTA.org

American Educational Research Association
http://aera.net

American Managed Behavioral Healthcare Association
www.ambha.org

American Psychiatric Association
www.psych.org

American Psychiatric Nurses Association
www.apna.org

American Psychoanalytic Association
http://apsa.org

American Psychological Association
www.apa.org

American Psychological Society
www.psychologicalscience.org

American Psychotherapy and Medical Hypnosis Associations
http://members.xoom.com/hypnosis

American Society of Clinical Hypnosis
www.ASCH.net

American Sociological Association
www.asanet.org

Applied Psychometric Society
www.fordham.edu/aps/index.html

Asian American Psychological Association
www.west.asu.edu:80/azamft

Association for Advanced Training in Behavioral Sciences
www.aatbs.com

Association for Death Education and Counseling
www.adec.org

Association for Humanistic Psychology
http://ahpweb.bestware.net/home.html

Association for Mental Health in Southern Portugal
www.terravista.pt/Enseada/1473

Association for Psychological Type
www.aptcentral.org
International organization for those interested in the study of personality types.

Association for Specialists in Group Work
http://blues.fdl.uc.edu/~wilson/asgw

Association for the Advancement of Gestalt Therapy
www.g~g.org/aagt

Association for the Advancement of Psychology
www.aapnet.org

Association for the Study of Dreams
www.asdreams.org

Association for Transpersonal Psychology
www.igc.org/atp

Association of Belgian Behavior Therapists
www.

Association of Black Psychologists
www.abpsi.org

Association of Sports Psychology
www.uni-leipzig.de/~asp/english.htm

Australian Psychological Society
www.psychsociety.com.au

Belgian Psychological Society
www.ulb.ac.be/bps

Biofeedback Foundation of Europe
www.bfe.org

British Association for Behavioral and Cognitive Psychotherapies
www.babcp.org.uk

British Psychological Society
www.bps.org.uk

Canadian Mental Health Association
www.icomm.ca/cmhacan

Canadian Psychiatric Association
http://cpa.medical.org/cpa/cpa.html

Canadian Psychoanalytic Society
http://homeican.net/~analyst

Canadian Psychological Association
www.cpa.ca

Eastern Psychological Association
www.easternpsychological.org

European Brief Therapy Association
http://html.passagen.se/solution/ebta.htm

European Health Psychology Society
www.ehps.net

Federation of Behavioral, Psychological and Cognitive Sciences
www.am.org/federation

German Psychological Society
www.dgps.de/dgps_english.html

International Association for Statistics Education
www.stat.ncsu.edu/info/iase

International Association of Applied Psychology
www.ucm.es/info/Psyap/iaap

International Association of Cognitive Psychotherapy
www.personal.kent.edu/~iacp

International Association of Group Psychotherapy
www.psych.mcgill.ca/labs/iagp/IAGP.html

International Association of Marriage and Family Counselors
http://familycounselors.org

International Federation of Social Workers
www.ifsw.org

International Neuropsychological Society
www.med.ohio-state.edu/ins/index.html

International Society for Theoretical Psychology
www.yorku.ca/dept/psych/orgs/istp/istp.htm

International Society for Political Psychology
www.ispp.org

International Stress Management Association
www.stress.org.uk/isma

International Transactional Analysis Association
www.itaa~net.org

Irish Association of Social Workers
http://homepage.iol.ie/~iasw

Israel Psychological Association
http://freud.tau.ac.il/~ipa

Italian Psychoanalytic Society
www.sicap.it/~merciai/spi.htm

Japan Clinical Psychology Association
www.bekkoame.or.jp/~koumi/gakai-e.htm

Midwestern Psychological Association
www.ssc.msu.edu/~mpa

National Association of Alcohol & Drug Abuse Counselors
www.naadc.org

National Association of Cognitive-Behavioral Therapists
www.nacbt.org

National Association of Drama Therapists
www.nadt.org

National Association of School Psychologists
www.naspweb.org

National Autistic Society
www.oneworld.org/autism_uk

National Association of Social Workers
www.socialworkers.org

New Jersey Association of Mental Health Agencies
www.njamha.org

Society of Personality and Social Psychology
www.spsp.org

ADDITIONS? ERRORS?

The author's diligence may not have ensured that all legal and ethical words and terms related to mental health were included, nor can he guarantee that this dictionary is error free. Therefore, solicitation is herein being made for additions and corrections for the next edition of this publication.

Additions: _____

_____

_____

_____

_____

_____

_____

_____

_____

_____

Corrections: _____

_____

_____

_____

_____

_____

_____

_____

_____

_____

Please provide us the following information:

Name: _____

Title/Organization: _____

_____

Address: _____

_____

City/Town: _____

State: _____ Zip: _____

Phone number: _____

Email: _____

Please Return To:

C. Emmanuel Ahia, Ph.D., J.D.
Rider University Graduate School,
Counsel/School Psychology Programs
M-202
Lawrenceville, NJ 08648
Phone: (609) 896-5339 Fax: (609) 896-5364

ABOUT THE AUTHOR

C. Emmanuel Ahia, Ph.D., J.D., NCC, L.PC is an Associate Professor and Program Coordinator of the Ed.S. in Counseling program at Rider University Graduate School. He has a Ph.D. in Educational Psychology from Southern Illinois University, a J.D. degree from University of Arkansas School of Law, an M.A. in Interpersonal/Counseling Psychology from Wheaton College Graduate School, Wheaton, Illinois. Dr. Ahia's law practice focuses, above all, in the area of health, mental health, and family law. He is author of one of the American Counseling Association's (ACA) Legal Series (1993) on <u>Confidentiality</u>; author of the section on <u>Insanity defense</u> in Magil's Encyclopedia of Psychology (2003), and author of other articles in the area of ethical conflicts in Counseling. He holds a Diplomat status in Forensic Counseling awarded by American Academy for Forensic Counseling. He is a member of American Counseling Association, American Bar Association, Pennsylvania Bar Association, and American Academy for Forensic Counseling.